The JOY of
CYBERSEX

The JOY of CYBERSEX

A Guide for Creative Lovers

DEB LEVINE

BALLANTINE BOOKS
NEW YORK

A Ballantine Book
Published by The Ballantine Publishing Group

http://www.randomhouse.com

LIBRARY OF CONGRESS CATALOGING-IN-PUBLICATION DATA
Levine, Deb.
The joy of cybersex : a guide for creative lovers / Deb Levine. — 1st ed.
        p.   cm.
Includes index.
ISBN 0-345-42580-4 (alk. paper)
1. Computer sex.   2. Sex.   3. Web sites.   4. Online chat groups.
I. Title.
HQ23.L48   1998
306.7'0285—dc21   98-21013
                                                                         CIP

Cover design by Barbara Leff
Cover photo © Barnaby Hall/Photonica
Text design by Holly Johnson

Manufactured in the United States of America

First Edition: September 1998

10   9   8   7   6   5   4   3   2   1

C O N T E N T S

ACKNOWLEDGMENTS

This book would not have been possible without the support, encouragement, and guidance of my agents and friends, Jandy Nelson and Jillian Manus of the Manus Literary Agency. The folks who read chapters in their barest form were amazingly good sports, and I thank them for exhuming their editing skills: Dawn Beckley, Will Hermes, Joan Meyers, and Maggie Sale. In addition, Thrive Partners, Inc. gave me the platform to develop my on-line persona, *Delilah,* and to use the Internet as an educational venue for conveying information about sexuality and relationships. My boss, David Markus, has been a mentor, as well as a source of wisdom and inspiration in my professional development. Many thanks to my editor at Ballantine Books, Amy Scheibe, for taking the risk of publishing a print book about cyberspace. Bob Madey has been my best friend and confidant, getting me to the point where I believed in myself enough to put my experiences into writing. And, of course, many thanks to my friends and family who saw me through my reclusive weekends of writing in the fall of 1997.

INTRODUCTION

Do you know which word is searched most often on the Internet? You've got it—SEX. But have *you* ever visited a sex site on the Web? I imagine you use your computer for personal and business e-mail, and maybe a little fancy word processing and database management. Sex sites on the Web have crossed your mind, but not your computer screen. Guess what? It's time to break the taboo and forge a path to the wealth of valuable sex information in cyberspace. Then you can learn how to apply it to your love, life, and relationships.

I've been working on the Net for more than five years. When I first began publishing as Alice, of the renowned **Go Ask Alice!** Web site (http://www.goaskalice.columbia.edu/index.html), not many people even knew what the Web was. (Hard to imagine these days, isn't it?) My job was to educate small groups of Ivy League students about the health issues said to concern them: sexual assault, HIV/AIDS, sexually transmitted diseases, and body image concerns. To keep their attention, I had to do just about everything except take off my clothes. After my hundredth or so lecture in the dorms, I realized these nightly group encounters were no longer effective with the MTV generation.

At my wit's end, I turned to my friends in the computer lab and suggested we create something on-line to reach the masses. In 1991, the Internet was for computer nerds, academicians, and engineers. The material available to the general public consisted largely of library holdings and administrative information. We were clearly breaking new ground with the service I proposed—teaching students about sensitive health concerns (and, of course, sex) via the Internet.

Having little computer experience didn't stop me. I learned quickly about the technology and how to convey information through cyberspace in an interesting, honest, and fun way. I answered health questions for three years in the name of Alice—questions as diverse as how long the average guy lasts in bed to how to handle an ingrown toenail. I received thousands of questions, and responded to over 750—most of which were about sex and relationships. It was obvious the world was interested in sex, but had nowhere to turn to get their answers.

The Net was the right place then, even more so now. It offers anonymity—something in-person lectures and workshops don't. It offers a level of honesty that is hard to get from your friends, lovers, or doctors. There is no one on the Net judging you for what you don't know, no one second-guessing whether you're a "normal" player in the sexual arena.

Today I'm answering your sex and relationship questions on-line as **Delilah@Thrive** (http://www.thriveonline.com/ sex/delilah.today.html). To date, I've posted more than 300 Q&As, and the answers are getting richer and more interesting every day. The questions: Am I normal? Am I good in bed? And the answers: If there's a person, place, or thing out there in the world, there's someone who gets turned on by it. And yes, you're normal.

You have a chance to find romance, revive your relationship, and explore fantasies in the relative safety and obscurity of cyberspace. If you haven't spent much time surfing for sex information, you'll be quite surprised at the variety, depth, and breadth of what's available. Shame and embarrassment are removed from the equation—the playing field is level. You get a chance to find out who you are sexually—what you really need and desire—and to bring it back to your real-life relationships in a healthy way.

The Joy of Cybersex explores the art of the possible in terms of sex on the Net. Each chapter contains a wealth of information:

- What you can do on-line to enhance your sex life.
- Great sites to visit with everything you need to know about how to navigate through them.
- Case studies of people who have used the sexual services offered in cyberspace.

Researchers say people who discuss sexuality openly and are comfortable with their bodies are better lovers and life partners. My goal in writing *The Joy of Cybersex* is to give you the chance to take advantage of what the Internet has to offer, and provide you with the tools for satisfying, lifelong sex.

Please note: Some of the Internet addresses listed in this book are likely to change by the time you read this. This is only natural in the fast-paced world of cyberspace. If you come across an error message while on-line, use your search engine to find the new URL (address) for a site, or sites of a similar nature more recently created.

The author in no way guarantees the nature or the validity of the content on the sites listed. The listings are simply examples of the variety of sites you might find on the Internet, not necessarily the best or most accurate.

CHAPTER ONE

EMERGING FROM YOUR SHELL

Sex and relationships are inextricably intertwined. While it's possible to have one without the other, it's not always a satisfying experience. If you're in a relationship and want to explore your sexuality in depth, skip right to Chapter Three: Explore Your Sexual Self. But if you're simply too shy even to consider the possibility of being intimate, then the Internet is a good place to learn and practice your social graces. This chapter is for you.

Everyone says you have to be "out there" in order to meet your special someone. And you have to risk rejection in order to enjoy the possibility of being accepted. They're right. But what if you can't bear the thought of walking up to a stranger, no less an attractive one, and saying something clever off the top of your head? Are you the kind of person who meets someone you find interesting, but then can't think of what to say or do to make a lasting impression? Or are you the guy or gal who always hears those dreaded words: "I just want to be friends"? Yes? You'd be surprised at how many people are in the same boat. If you find it incredibly difficult to begin an intimate relationship, don't despair. The Internet can serve as a training ground to help you practice your flirting skills (anonymously), make mistakes (and learn from them!), find support, and build your self-confidence.

Negative self-talk ("She'd only reject me" or "He'd think I was such an idiot") will only take you down the road away from love. We all know that it's unlikely you'd die if you spoke to an attractive stranger, even if you did stutter or say something stupid. And that it won't be the end of the world if you get rejected once or twice. Although it may seem unbelievable, everyone who's currently coupled has been there, done that.

But it does take confidence and motivation to get over self-defeating thoughts. And it takes some basic skills in negotiating dialogue when you meet a new person. While every magazine on the stand has tips and advice for how to date and relate, it's a one-sided affair—you read the article, then you put the magazine down. The beauty of the Internet is that it's interactive—there are places to read the advice, then practice the new skills you've read about with real people, and field your mistakes (and successes!) with other folks in an anonymous, supportive environment. The fluidity of the medium lends an experiential quality to your learning that's not possible with print. The anonymity creates an environment where you can make mistakes without feeling embarrassed or ashamed. You'll find the support you need to keep on building skills until you're confident and satisfied.

In the privacy of your own home, you can get the advice and support you need to overcome your shyness. You can even practice flirting with strangers in your pajamas! No one will ever know if you haven't slept a wink, if you have stubble on your face, or if you haven't put on your makeup yet. In addition to not having to worry about looking your best, the anonymity also means you never have to see a particular person again if you flub it. If at first you don't succeed, you can try, try again, and no one will ever know.

In this chapter, I'll tell you how you can use the Internet to:

- Find the best places to practice flirting
- Learn to be a star-studded flirt
- Build skills to take with you on the road
- Create an on-line support system to overcome your shyness
- Turn your romantic life from "I just want to be friends" into "I think I'm in love!"

Before we get started, let's find out if you're already a flirt. Whether or not you know it, there are things we do that other people find flirtatious or, conversely, standoffish. Half the time, we're not even conscious that we're sending out these signals. But if you want to be successful in the world of love, it's important to start paying attention to your body language and your words. Assess your current status as a flirt: Take a few minutes to answer these questions about yourself (honestly!).

You see someone in the grocery store who is incredibly attractive. You:
 ____ a) Follow him or her around the store with your cart, but don't dare approach. (4)
 ____ b) Think about the person while you're shopping and the whole way home. You spend the afternoon kicking yourself for not saying anything. (2)
 ____ c) Spend some time thinking of an opening line, and at the checkout, walk up to him or her and test it out. (6)

You're attracted to a good friend. But that's all you've been for a long time—friends. You're both single now, so the coast is clear. You call him or her up to:
 ____ a) Make a date to catch up on your lives. (4)
 ____ b) Go out for dinner in a romantic restaurant. (6)
 ____ c) Say "Hi" and see what happens. (2)

You go to a party alone. You get there and realize you know only a few people. You:
 ____ a) Head over to the people you know and start a conversation. (2)
 ____ b) Chitchat your way to the bar to get a drink, then smilingly wind your way to the food. (4)

___ c) Find someone who looks interesting, seat yourself near them, and start talking. (6)

An attractive person comes up to you while you're reading on the bus and says, "That looks like a fascinating book. Do you like it?" You:

___ a) Scowl and change seats. (2)

___ b) Make eye contact, tell him or her you love it, and ask if they want to see the cover. (6)

___ c) Say "Yes" with a hint of a smile on your face. (4)

Add up your points and see how you've scored.

8–12 You have some work to do. Flirting is an art, and you have to know how to both give and receive sexy signals. Unfortunately, most of the signals you give off say, "Don't even think about trying to talk to me." You could stand to build some skills in the subtle art of flirting. Read on and you'll get a good dose of advice and info from the Net to help you gain confidence and become comfortable meeting new people.

13–18 You're a flirt by inspiration! That means you have it in you, but you don't always use what you've got. Read on for some new ideas to inspire you. Then get out there and start practicing, first on the Net, then in real life. There's someone out there just waiting to flirt with you.

19–24 You're a natural-born flirt. If you're single, you're not at a loss for dates, and if you're in a relationship or married, your partner is a happy soul because you know how to keep the fires stoked. You can skip this chapter and head right into the next one. Oh, and don't forget that many folks out there could learn a thing or two from you, so be sure to set a good example. Happy flirting!

Now you know where you stand; it's time to take a lesson from the pros and learn how to become a successful flirt.

LOCATION, LOCATION, LOCATION

All the advice people give about flirting is true. You can flirt anytime, anywhere, anyplace, and have fun (and potentially meet someone great!). Places you'd never thought of to flirt—like the service station, a movie theater line, or in your computer class—are the most likely places that you'll meet someone with common interests. The same holds true on the Internet.

While there are sites geared specifically to flirting, you're best off finding a chat room or an on-line community that revolves around a subject you're interested in—sports, health, kids, books. Hang around to see if anyone participating in the conversation strikes your fancy. **America Online** has chat rooms in the People Connection (the hub of AOL chat) with names like Artists' Café, Authors' Lounge, Movie Madness, Shy Friends, Careers and Family, Christian Fellowship, College Corner, Divorced, Over 40, Philosophy, Single Parents, Extreme Sports, Media, Astrology, Around the World, Great Outdoors, Born Again, Garden, Pet Chat, Romance, Recovery, and more.

Beware, some room titles are deceptive. One night I visited a variety of rooms. There really were authors in the Authors' Lounge, and the Great Outdoors chat topic was backpacking, but the Movie Madness chat room was a bunch of hormonally charged teenagers talking nonsense. *C'est la vie.*

On the Web, you can find large (and I mean large) chat communities on **Yahoo** (http://www.yahoo.com), **Excite/ Webcrawler** (http://www.excite.com/channel/chat/), **Talk City** (http://www.talkcity.com), and **Internet Relay Chat** (IRC) (http://www.mirc.com/). Each has its own software, and all except IRC load automatically while you sit and watch. On most of the sites, you need to choose a chat name. You can change this as many times as you like (good for when you stick your virtual foot in your virtual mouth), or you can keep your name and password stored in a safe place so that you can use it whenever you visit the site.

Yahoo's hottest chat rooms on the nights I visited were Music, Thirties, Forties, GenX Love, Teen Love, 30's Love, and Married & Flirting. On Excite, there were over 5,000 people chatting, 25 to a room, in rooms categorized by age group, geographic location, and topics such as autos, books, computers, film, games, health, lifestyles, music, politics, sports, TV, and travel. Talk City had close to 4,000 chatters in rooms with names like TheInSite, LatinoChat, New2TalkCity, ArtCity, BookTalk, CityPub, FoodTalk, MusicTalk, ParentChat, Sailing, and SciFi.

IRC takes a bit more technological savvy, as you have to manually download the software, execute it, and then sign on to a server site. (Don't worry, it sounds more complicated than it is.) IRC was the first chat software available, long before most of us had even heard of the World Wide Web. It's user-friendly, and on a 28.8 modem it doesn't take all that long to set up.

The folks chatting on IRC tend to be technologically savvy and sophisticated about computers. Up to 2,000 people can chat at the same time in the same channel (the IRC equivalent of chat rooms), so the anonymity factor is great. You can choose from channels like Friends-N-Flirts or Computer Networking (or thousands of others), and most are quite friendly. Depending on the channel, things can get busy and hectic. But it's a great place to observe and find out about the pace and the gestalt of chat before you jump in.

Your best bet is to pick a room or channel on any of the sites mentioned above and then head in to see what's going on. Flirting takes a different form in cyberspace, of course, since all the vital aspects of "nonverbals" are absent. All that means, though, is that the remaining methods of flirtation—language, timing, and, yes, flattery—are heightened. Used sparingly, "emoticons" (smileys and winks) and narrative asides like <LOL> (laughing out loud) can add sizzle to on-line chats. Here's a quick primer of some of the more common things you'll "hear" in a chat room. Most have been developed as a sort of shorthand, to keep you from having to type the same phrases over and over again.

LOL	laughing out loud
ROFL	rolling on floor laughing
LMAO	laughing my ass off
IMHO	in my humble opinion
BRB	be right back
AFK	away from keyboard
IM	instant message (AOL)
ICQ	instant message (Web software)

In addition, there are what are often called "emoticons." These are symbols created with characters from your keyboard to reflect emotions, discernible if you turn your head 90 degrees to the left and use a little imagination.

;) winking
:p sticking one's tongue out
:} smiling

People get very creative with their designs—adding mustaches and other identifying features to their "faces." It's a personal style thing.

You may also notice designs in the chat rooms. They're called "macros"—picture images made up of symbols and characters that take up more than one line of chat. Thanks to THRVStarr, here are some examples:

```
       ;;;;;;;;;;;;
       ;;;;;’_____;’
       ;;;(/)))))I((\
      _;;(((((((I))))
       / I_\\\\\\\\\\\
  .---~( \~)))))))))))))
   /    \ ’\-(((((((((((\ \
   I   I ’\  ) I \        /I)
   I   I ‘._/ _____/ I
   I   ,’\~           /
   I    \ \          /
   I ‘.  ’\I        /
   I ~-  ‘\      /
   \____~._/~ -_, {S smooch}
    I   I :;;;’    \
    I /  I          I
    I   I          I
    I  ‘.       /
```

```
==========ₒₒ0=======0ₒₒ========/A Big
‡‡‡‡‡‡‡‡‡‡‡‡‡‡‡‡‡§§§  ‡‡‡‡‡‡‡‡‡‡‡‡‡‡/KiŠŠ
‡‡‡‡‡‡‡‡‡‡‡‡‡‡‡‡ {ô¿ô}  ‡‡‡‡‡‡‡‡‡‡‡‡‡‡/ Right
‡‡‡‡‡‡‡‡‡‡‡‡‡‡‡‡ ¥ ‡‡‡‡‡‡‡‡‡‡‡‡‡/ Through The
‡‡‡‡‡‡‡‡‡‡‡‡‡‡‡‡‡‡‡‡‡‡‡‡‡‡‡‡‡‡‡‡‡‡‡‡/ Screen!
                         {S Kiss}
```

People also exchange "wavs," or sound files. You can tell someone's sent one (if you don't have the software to hear them) because they show up on-screen as something like {S giggle (a bracket in front of a word or phrase, as {smooch and {kiss in the macros above). The range of sounds is quite tremendous, from the sound of a smack on the lips to a guffaw to heavy breathing. You need to have speakers and sound file software installed on your computer to hear these clearly.

Some software (like iChat, the most common one found on the Web these days) also has "word emotions," so that you can click an emotion from a list and what appears on-screen is something like, "SpringChicken is awe-inspired by your thoughts." (You are SpringChicken in this scenario, in case you were wondering.) On some of the sites you can also change the color of your text and background to emphasize phrases or sentences.

Most areas have guides and help commands so that you can learn the particulars. Sites on the Net are getting more and more user-friendly, as they're trying to encourage people to feel comfortable chatting. As I mentioned before, IRC has the most technological instructions, whereas some of the sites that are running Java applets (that's a little application) are unqualifiably simple.

Go into a room and observe how people use their on-line tools to flirt. While it may seem ridiculous, I'm sure you'll find it amazing how much coquetry and emotion people can convey on-line when they are skilled and willing.

STAR-STUDDED FLIRTING

Just as in real life, there is an art to flirting on-line. It involves knowing some of the chat etiquette, but it also involves developing your social skills. As in real life, people will let you know *very* quickly if you're out of line. Unlike in real life, you can then change your screen name, reenter, and give it another shot. And no one will know it was you who made that giant faux pas. You can even try flirting again with the same person!

The Internet is a wonderful place to practice flirting and to learn social graces because it's anonymous. With thousands of people chatting every night on various sites, you can surf the rooms casually, test out your "moves," and meet a host of different people. This should give you the courage to do the same in your daily life, once you realize most people would be more likely to talk to you if you start a conversation than if you hang around nervously without saying a word.

Here are a few tips to get you psyched up for the brave new world of flirting on the Net:

IT'S ALL IN A NAME. Choose a great nickname or screen name. Pick something that doesn't carry any double meaning you don't intend. For instance, I once chose the name HealthHeroine, meant as the female form of hero, but it was perceived as the drug, even though it's spelled differently. Being mistaken for a drug addict did not get me very many dates!

Gendered names work better for flirting, because they

make it easier for people to decide whether to approach. You want to be quippy, funny, and attention-getting in two words or less. Try out a few different names and see if you like the kind of attention you get. (Oh, and women, don't use the word *sexy* in your name, or you'll be bombarded. Men, don't mention sex in your name, or any sexual references—women will avoid you like the plague.)

OBSERVE, THEN MAKE YOUR MOVE. Watch the conversation in a particular room for a while. See who you find interesting, funny, or attractive. Choose that person to address when you are ready to enter the discussion.

OPENING-LINE COOL. Your first line is important, but don't agonize over it. With the revolving door in most chat rooms, you'll have a second chance. An easy choice is to ask the person you think is clever his or her age and where they live. This is a common tool used in chat rooms to establish an initial connection. Your other option is to jump into the conversation, on topic, of course, and ask a question of one of the prime players, or the room as a whole. Once you start chatting, others in the room will notice you and hopefully take initiative.

BE POLITE, GET INTIMATE. Use the screen name of the person you're speaking to when you address them. Either start your sentence with their name, or end with it for emphasis. "Luv2Cuddle, I thought *The Piano* was a great movie, too. Don't you think Jane Campion is brilliant?"

Here's an excerpt from a flirtatious time in a chat:

GUEST1: I love kissing. Is that too woozey for a guy?

GUEST2: Guest1, no, that's cool!

GUEST3: It can improve your relationship if it's done right and in the right places.

GUEST4: Yes, I think it's great when a guy is totally into kissing!

GUEST1: Good, my friends think it is a waste of time.

GUEST4: Tell them they're all wet! Kissing has many fantastic features. . . . Very sensual, it demonstrates a very heightened sensitivity, I think.

GUEST1: I agree, they don't know what they're missing. I think it is a language of affection without words.

GUEST4: You can say so much without speaking, Guest1.

GUEST1: You are talking, but in a different way.

Do you think these two are going to get together or what? There was no direct pickup happening, just a gentle discussion of a sensual act they both appreciate. Notice that conversation among the other guests dropped off pretty quickly. I imagine those two headed off to a private chat room called "Into the Sunset."

FORUM FORAYS

You can also flirt in on-line forums, sometimes called message boards. The difference between chats and boards is that chats are in real time, and you have only a sentence or two to make your point. The good thing about chats is that give-and-take is immediate. On the boards, you can think about what you want to say, and edit your words before you make your message public. You also have a chance to see how people respond to you without any public face time. You may want to start flirting on the boards because it's less intimidating, then graduate to chats.

Here are some samples of flirting from the America Online boards. Note how the act of describing the art of flirting is a subtle flirtation in and of itself.

> *Subject: The art of the spoken word . . .*
> *Looking for ladies who enjoy being pampered with good conversation and the sensuality of the spoken word. Well-thought conversation is an art, and its appreciation is an extraordinary gift! I love to talk about anything and everything, so if you're interested in avoiding the immature, crass babble on-line and having a great talk, please e-mail me or look for me on-line. . . .*

> *Subject: Open me with words*
> *I'm interested in people whose words can soothe the savage beast. If you have a romantic imagination and think you can sweep my heart away with your words, try me.*

> *Subject: It's an art*
> *Flirting is more than "Hi, ya wanna?" It's teasing, playing, innuendos—it's about making someone feel*

special, it's about being attentive, it's about walking on the edge of danger & getting caught. Flirting is nibbling on the forbidden fruit. It's not blunt straight-to-the-point comments. It's playing cat & mouse with each other, and enjoying it.

TAKING IT ON THE ROAD

Here's the good news. On-line flirting works best when it is used hand in hand with real-life flirting; each one picks up where the other leaves off. If you've been flirting on-line with someone for a while, by the time you meet in person, you'll have enough tidbits of info about him to flirt with finesse. Nervousness aside, you've already cut through the small talk and gotten past the "What should I say first?" stage.

However, this familiarity can also make you feel so comfortable that you forget the reality of the situation. If you've met the person only in the virtual world, all you know about him is what he's chosen to tell you. In some cases, it won't be a problem; in others, what she's chosen not to write about can be very telling (and disappointing).

Here's another way to go about the whole thing: Once you become comfortable with your flirting skills on-line, practice them with someone you know in real life but have been too timid to approach. This is the ultimate test, and a perfect way to use the medium to your advantage. Take this course: You meet someone in real life whom you find interesting. You go on-line to try out a few first lines and pump up your confidence with strangers. You use your newfound confidence to send a "flirty" e-mail to the real-life person. She responds in the affirmative. Now you're ready to take your skills on the road and see how you fare face-to-face.

The heart of true flirting takes place in conversation— that is, what gets said—or what *almost* gets said. Even when talking about a neutral topic, you can use the conversation to flirt. Pick terms that sound sexy—describe a film you recently saw as "out of control" or use words like "sensuous, juicy, and delectable" to describe the meal you just finished.

Good flirting involves interaction between two people. You've got to pay attention and respond to your flirting partner. It's not hard to forget, because you're naturally flirting with someone you're attracted to. The key is this: Your flirting counts ten times as much if it is done in response to your flirtee. Remember, the idea is that you're doing it together, to see if you're well suited for being partners in a deeper, more intimate way.

It takes confidence to believe that your crush is really flirting and not just "being nice." As Susan Rabin, a self-professed master flirt, says, "Don't be your own worst enemy." Trust your judgment. Listen to yourself. Until you receive real communication to the contrary, keep your spirits high and move things along.

There are a few sites on-line where you can pick up real-life flirting tips, advice, and information. The most extensive site is **Flirts International** (http://www.flirts.com). Although the site is not interactive in any way, it is "*dedicated to the principle that flirting is a delightful, innocent, re-*

spectful way to play with each other." It espouses creative flirting and offers frank, practical ways to attain social ease in these edgy times. The Angel of Flirting answers your questions with smart, rational advice, and you can find articles such as "Being Attractive," which begins with the opening line from *Gone with the Wind: "Scarlett O'Hara was not beautiful, but men seldom realized it when caught by her charm."* There is a funny list of famous flirts and non-flirts (Bill Clinton falling into the flirt category; Hillary Clinton into the nonflirt . . .), tips for flirting with your spouse or lover, and an article on creative kissing. Nothing to lose by visiting this site; lots to gain. It's well worth a visit.

You can find **Tips for Successful Cyber-Flirting** at the LoveLife site (http://www.lovelife.com/flirt-woman.html or flirt-man.html). Each site includes ten tips to teach you how to flirt with a man or woman on the Net, including such highlights as "Treat a woman well" and "Be friends first" for men and "Seduction happens in stages" and "Men need visual stimulation" for women. This site also boasts an area filled with cyberlove stories. From successful marriages to broken hearts, this is the place where you'll hear it all.

CupidNet (http://www.cupidnet.com) is a comprehensive, up-to-the-minute listing of sites for singles on the Web. It is very well organized by geographic region and by medium (on-line or real life). The listings of local singles events are the best out there, so if you're looking for something in your neighborhood, this site is a great resource.

If you want to try your luck kissing an attractive

stranger before you head out on a date, check out the **Virtual Kissing Booth** (http://www.whitehawk.com/vkb). Each month, one man and one woman are profiled in the booth. You can take a peek at the photos (most of them are puckered up!), read bios, and send e-mail explaining why you'd want to kiss him or her, complete with details on how you'd go about doing it. You can also nominate yourself (or your best friend!) to be the monthly "kisser."

Another handy on-line resource is the **Fantastic Books, Cassettes, and Videos on How to Successfully Meet, Attract, and Seduce Women** site, otherwise known as **Get Girls** (http://www.getgirls.com). While the name is a bit much, you can find an excellent catalog of off-line resources, weekly flirting tips, and chapters from the authors' books, *A Man's Guide to Women* and *How to Seduce Hot and Sexy Beautiful Women.* The tips are quite funny, albeit a bit sexist at times, so beware if you're easily offended.

On a more serious note, one site operated by Mental Health Net is a plethora of **Resources for the Shy** (http://www.cmhc.com/guide/selfestm.htm). It includes on-line brochures (complete with thumbs-up, thumbs-down user ratings and starred site ratings), links to on- and off-line resources, and products to help you overcome your shyness. The brochures are from universities as well as private psychotherapy clinics, and range from titles such as "Shyness" to "Fifty Ways to Increase Your Self-Esteem" to "The Social Support and Loneliness Home Page." Products include written affirmations and stickers. There is also a link to a singles newsgroup (soc.singles). However, when I followed the link, I found it read more like a college sociology course, complete with feminist arguments, than a place for social support or flirting.

America Online has a good flirting area at **Thrive@ Passion** (Keyword: @Passion). You'll find tips and advice for how to give and send sexy signals, flirt with a partner, and flirt on-line. There's also a happening forum with topics such as Flirting Tips and Tricks, Flirting Advice, Flirt Buddies, and more. Some selections from the boards follow:

Subject: I need help
I'm usually an outgoing person, but when I meet someone I'm attracted to, my natural persona kinda disappears. I try too hard to make a good first impression, and I forget what a wonderful person I am and can be. How can I show the world, and the guys I want to date, what a great person I am without looking like I'm blowing my own horn or I'm a complete goober? Anyone with any advice or good self-esteem-boosting tips is welcome to write anytime. Thanks so much.

Subject: Re: I need help
Guys like babes who are themselves—just show that beautiful person you are and you'll be fine. You're the kind of girl I dig, just let that beauty shine. Take care Sugar.

Subject: Need Help for Shy People
Hi! I'm really really, really shy. Flirting . . . well, I

*stink at it. I feel awkward flirting with a guy, espe-
cially the one I'm in love with. Even making eye contact is difficult for me. HELP!! I don't know what to
do. How do I get over being nervous, let alone flirt?*

Subject: Re: Need Help for Shy People
*I was extremely shy in my younger days, but I did get
"the guy." I always happened to be going in the opposite direction he was going at the same time, and as we
passed each other, I slowed down just enough to look
him in the eye and smile. Then I looked shyly away.
We dated for eight years and have now been married
eleven. A smile does it EVERY time! Good luck!*

WITH A LITTLE HELP FROM MY FRIENDS

As is true in so many other communities (chronic ills,
weight loss, disabilities, etc.), people who are trying to overcome shyness have found a safe home on the Internet.
When you feel overwhelmed by the thought of meeting
someone new, or you've just stuck your foot in your mouth
for the umpteenth time, it's natural to turn to the anonymous environment of the Net for confidence and support.

While the chat rooms are great for practicing your flirting skills, the real-time aspect of the rooms doesn't lend itself to finding support for your efforts. Sometimes you
want to have more of a discussion about the ins and outs of
flirting, and a willing ear to commiserate about your real
and virtual flirting experiences. Message boards and news-

groups can provide the medicine you need. There are no restrictions on how much you can write in these venues, and people can choose to respond to your dilemma or to read on.

At the **Shyness Support newsgroup** (sign up at http://www.tile.net/news/altsupportshyness.html), there are over 6,500 readers a day, and approximately eleven new messages posted daily. You can either read the messages on the Web, or have them delivered to your e-mail box. Responses can be posted publicly to the newsgroup, or sent privately to the author. Recent topics in this newsgroup included When is a date a date?, Went to the Gym and . . . , Crisis of Confidence, and Dealing with. . . . Here are some selections from this newsgroup so you can get an idea of the depth of support you might find:

Subject: Crisis of confidence

I'm finding myself having the biggest confidence crisis since I started to shake off my shyness. I find myself feeling so depressed so much of the time. Depressed that I can't tell people how I really feel about them, depressed that I don't have a girlfriend (this and the previous might go together, I suspect), depressed that I refuse promotion opportunities at work, depressed that I can't show confidence. . . . I know that it all boils down to the shyness thing, but I just can't do anything to shake it off. Can you ever cure a severe case of shyness 100%, or are you always going to feel weird about doing certain stuff?

Then there's women. Well, woman, more to the point. There's a girl who I've known well for the past 2 years. She's wonderful, but she's going through huge problems with the split-up of a relationship she was in almost a year ago. The problem is that when she wants to talk about it, more often than not, she comes to me. Don't get me wrong, I value every conversation, because I really think that I can help just by being there and injecting some logic into her situation . . . even if she never follows my advice.

She's one of the few people that makes me feel comfortable, and we can end up talking for hours about nothing. After we leave each other, I feel invigorated and happy because I know that I (Mr. Shy-guy) have had a good, long, meaningful conversation with someone. But then the next day I start to feel terrible, basically because (and you could probably see this coming) I find her attractive. Of course, she's never so much as hinted at any interest in me.

So the crunch question is: Should I establish where I stand by coming right out with how I feel? Or should I guess by the fact that she doesn't seem to look at me in a romantic light that she's just not interested? And if the latter applies, how do I handle the fact that she will never be more than a friend?

Oh well, I think I need to sleep now.

Subject: Re: Crisis of confidence

Well, you can take comfort in the fact that you don't *have* to tell people how you feel about them, and actually, it's usually better not to. When trying to promote change in your life, if it's just a matter of "I always do X but I want to do Y," it's actually a fairly straightforward process to recondition yourself. It takes maybe ten minutes. People consistently achieve this with hypnosis/NLP (neurolinguistic programming).

However, I find with shy people, it's almost always more complicated, because they don't know exactly what changes they want to make. They may be sick of being the way they are, but they don't have a complete, working model of something better to move toward.

Since I'm going to assume you don't have a hunchback or horns growing out of your head or anything like that, here are some things for you to think about:

1) There are very specific behaviors that cause women to become attracted to and interested in a man (and vice versa). Perhaps you don't use them.

2) There could be any number of women in the past who noticed you and sent you some kind of signal, hoping against hope that you'd pick up on it and pay attention to them, only you were oblivious to it all. This is often characteristic of people who are very introspective and self-conscious; they're so preoccupied with their own thoughts that they have little or no awareness of what others are feeling and the signals they're sending.

You should NOT just come right out and tell this woman how you feel. If you're determined to have romantic relations with this girl, you have to somehow get her to seriously consider you in that way WITHOUT overwhelming her with a sudden declaration of your feelings. The idea has to grow on her gradually, and she has to think it was HER idea, not yours.

No small task, by any means, but not impossible. If you think you can pull it off, go for it! Otherwise, take some time to cool off, maybe not talk to her at all for a while, until you're focused on someone else and you can honestly meet her at the friendship level.

Subject: Re: Crisis of confidence

Thank you for your advice. You may have prevented me from making a complete arse of myself tomorrow night (a party where the two of us would have been together). Of course you're right. I've actually been at the receiving end of this sort of thing. And if the feeling isn't mutual, then you can easily get very pissed off with the other person. I suppose I should have remembered this, but I didn't. It took you to re-mind me. Thanks.

It's clear there are times when you're struggling with an issue and you don't need the help of a therapist, or friends who can't be objective. You need someone who doesn't know you, but who's been through it before. The Net forums can be just the cure for what ails you.

NO MORE "JUST FRIENDS"

You're best friends with the person you want to become romantically involved with, and you're dating someone you could care less about (or not dating at all). You have the shoulder that women love to cry on, and of course they're beautiful women who are dating creeps. You are the nice guy, and feel like you're forever doomed to this role.

Believe it or not, there are ways to break out of this pattern. You can learn to become the romantic, the one people want to date. You have to start by learning to send the right signals—sensuous signals, sexy signals. Signals that make it clear to the other person what kind of relationship you're interested in. If you just sit back and wait for your friend to "get it," you make it easy for him to find love elsewhere.

How do you do this? Once you're sure you have romantic feelings, surprise your friend by doing something different. If you usually hang out together in jeans and a T-shirt at your house, plan on meeting in a romantic restaurant and get dressed up for the occasion next time you get together. If she usually comes over to your house to talk about her problems, make sure you have some sensuous music on and a bottle of wine nearby next time she arrives. If he's always talking about meeting the "wrong" kind of women, ask him point-blank what kind of woman he's looking for. When he starts describing your qualities—make no bones about it; tell him that you two would be perfect together.

While this all seems incredibly bold, the key to successful flirting and dating is that you'll never know if your offer will be accepted until you try. And we all have to risk a bit of rejection along the way. What you have to be gentle about, once you reveal your romantic feelings to a good friend, is not losing the friendship. When you suggest the option of being more than just friends, make sure you leave room for the other person to say no. If she doesn't feel cornered, it will be easier for her to let you know she's not interested in you "that way," and for the two of you to have a chance at continuing the friendship. Be ready to hear no, and try your best not to take it personally. Remember, you are considered her "best friend," and that's a pretty important role to play in someone's life.

A very effective and safe way to move a "just friends" relationship into romantic mode is to use e-mail. It's an easy opportunity to flirt your way into your friend's heart. The fact that you don't have to look someone straight in the eye can lend that all-important bit of courage you need to bring your real-life relationship one step closer to what you desire. Try this: At the end of an e-mail to your "friend," lose control and admit that "he nearly knocked you off your feet the other day." Then, at a quiet time alone soon afterward, tell your crush, "It's true what I said in my e-mail the other day." You may be well on your way to moving beyond flirting forever.

Don't forget there are two parts to flirting—sending the vibes and interpreting your flirting partner's signals. If you've put yourself on the line by saying he nearly knocked you off your feet, then you've got to hope it's taken the right way. If he responds, "What do you know about this new free e-mail I'm using? I kind of like it," it's time for you to take the hint and move on. When you see him in person after a response like that, smile and keep things on a superficial level. In your own mind, start thinking about whom to flirt with next. If, on the other hand, his response to your on-line flirting is, "I'm flattered. I'd love to knock you off your feet again—how about Wednesday?"—you're in the money. Take it away. Send the signals, read the response, and carry on.

CONCLUSION

While some people seem like natural-born flirts, the truth is, flirting techniques and skills can be learned. You have to put in some effort, just as you would with anything new. Now things are easier because of the added on-line option—risk-free flirting at your fingertips! The Internet offers advice and info, places to practice flirting and people to practice with, as well as peer support to get you through your flubs and fluffs. Melding your on-line flirting efforts with your real-life relationships can help you attract the people you want in your life, or up the ante in a friendship to a wonderful romantic encounter.

Now that you know all about flirting, how about some help finding someone to flirt with? If you've been too scared to get out there and meet new folks, or you've already dated (and rejected) everyone in town, the Internet offers an entirely new realm of potentials. Whether you're looking for a date, a commitment, or a no-strings-attached relationship, there are many, many people to meet in the virtual world. You just have to know how to navigate the course.

ANNOTATED SITE LISTING

Sites that maintain large chat communities:

http://www.yahoo.com Yahoo
http://www.excite.com/channel/chat
   Excite/Webcrawler
http://www.talkcity.com Talk City
http://www.mirc.com/ Internet Relay Chat (IRC)
http://www.flirts.com Flirts International offers
   frank, practical ways to attain social ease in these
   edgy times.
http://www.lovelife.com/flirt-woman.html or
   flirt-man.html Tips for Successful Cyber-Flirting

at the LoveLife site teaches you how to flirt on the Net, and has lots of testimonials from successful flirters.

http://www.cupidnet.com CupidNet is a comprehensive listing of sites for singles on the Web.

http://www.whitehawk.com/vkb The Virtual Kissing Booth is a silly site that profiles two people each month who are up for being kissed.

http://www.getgirls.com The How to Successfully Meet, Attract, and Seduce Women site offers an excellent catalog of off-line resources, weekly flirting tips, and chapters from the authors' books.

http://www.cmhc.com/guide/selfestm.htm Operated by Mental Health Net, this site has a wealth of resources for the shy.

AOL Keyword @Passion Thrive@Passion offers tips and advice for how to give and send flirting signals, how to flirt with a partner, and how to flirt on-line.

http://www.tile.net/news/altsupportshyness.html Sign up here for the Shyness Support newsgroup.

LOOKING FOR LOVE

My love and I met through Web personals in April 1996. We have lived together for the past 11 glorious months. Just thought you would like to know. And thanks.

I met my husband through an on-line service. We have quite an incredible story. A local group that is doing a documentary on interesting love stories has even asked to film us! Without the Web, I would never have known that my soul mate was searching for me in Alaska, over 3,500 miles away! He is now in WV and we are very happily married.

Who hasn't heard a story like this recently? But I bet you've also heard the tragedies—the woman who married a man who was really a woman; the stalker; the bilker; the list goes on. And it's all true. People have met on-line and married, and people have been taken for a ride. Just like in real life.

Sign on to the Web, and the door is open—many, many new possibilities of people to meet. People you never would have met because you couldn't bring yourself to go to the monthly church social, or the new dance club, or the latest invitation-only singles event in your town. Instead, in the privacy of your own home, you can surf the Web personals—complete with photos. Second only to meeting face-to-face to see if there's a spark, the Net offers you a safe place to explore and expand your dating horizons.

People sink huge sums of money into real-life dating services. Some charge $1,000 or more each year and guarantee that they'll find you a soul mate. And most of these services meet their guarantees. How? If two people are ready—they're in that place where they're both willing to commit to a relationship—and it so happens they meet, compatibility and love will naturally grow over time. So, if you're willing to invest $1,000 or more into a dating service, it's likely you're ready. (Hopefully, you're not desperate—simply ready to do the work, to know yourself inside and out, to meet someone compatible and make it happen.)

The on-line dating services are not that developed yet, and no one's charging $1,000 a pop. Most are free or charge a low monthly fee, and most do give you quick results. The on-line sites are basically an easily searchable database of personal ads. Think of it this way: Instead of having to buy a subscription to your local alternative weekly, regional daily paper, and urban monthly magazine to get a full complement of personal ads to choose from, you can simply go on-line and find a huge variety of ads at your fingertips. All the on-line services operate on the same premise—either you place a personal ad (often called a profile) and wait for people to respond to your "secret" e-mail address, or you search the available profiles and send e-mail to other people's secret addresses. It's that simple.

The trick is learning how to plow through the returns and find the silver dollar, keeping your wits about you in the process. In this chapter, I'll

- Tell you what qualities to look for in an on-line matchmaking service
- Point out the best current sites for on-line dating
- Teach you how to write a compelling personal ad or profile
- Give you pointers for which ads to respond to and which to DELETE
- Show you where to find sound cyberdating advice

But before we get into the nuts and bolts of finding love on-line, are you ready for a relationship? Consider the following questions:

- Did you just come out of a relationship?
- Do you know why your last relationship didn't work?
- Have you ever spent time alone without being lonely?
- Have you thought about the qualities that you'd like in a new partner?

- Are you familiar with what qualities you have to of-
  fer a new partner?
- What is your value system—Are you keen on family
  life? Is career a priority?
- How important is religion?
- Are you a political person?

Try the following exercise off-line. Be honest with
yourself and give it your best shot. List all the qualities you'd
like in a significant other. Think about your past relationships both in terms of what was good and what was
missing. Make sure you include things like physical characteristics, values, career, finances, communication skills,
personality, children, family, spiritual or religious beliefs.
Once you've exhausted the list, next to each trait, give it a
letter: **M** for *must have,* **G** for *you could give it up if you had
to,* and **C** for *willing to compromise.* Here's an example:

Tall C
Dark: Brown hair, brown eyes C
Holds a job C
Good-looking M
Independent M
World-traveled M
Well-read M
Intelligent M
Good communicator C
Sincere M
Sense of humor M
Respects his family M

Wants children (birth or adopted) M
Has to be able to support himself M
Likes cats G
Assertive C
Self-assured C
Honest M

Next time you meet a potential date, *don't hold her to the test on the first date!* That would be unfair, and cause you to have many first dates without any follow-up. But as you get to know a person, check your list every once in a while. Make sure you're not compromising on your must-haves, and you're not insisting on things you're really willing to give up.

They say love is blind—and you know what? The first few weeks or months after you fall in starry-eyed love, you *are* blind. And that's when you're most likely to make compromises you'll later regret. So take this little exercise seriously—be clear and honest with yourself about your priorities, and stick by them. You're more likely to get what you want if you know what you want. Know what I mean? Now, let's get down to the meaty stuff.

THE SERVICE COUNTS

All dating services are not alike. This is especially true on-line, where the sheer volume of people causes different types to flock to different sites. Some sites attract younger folks, some attract professional careerists, some attract people searching for romance, and others seeking sex. It's hard to tell exactly who you'll find on any particular site at first glance.

If you search for romance, dating services, or cyberlove on the Net, you'll come up with a huge list. Don't just choose the first one in desperation, or the one with the name you like best. Choose a few sites and administer the following *Joy of Cybersex* test. Take your time making a decision. If you find the right site(s) for you, you're more likely to meet someone compatible.

Most sites operate like the personal ads in newspapers. The advantage to the on-line services is a built-in search mechanism so you can easily find the type of people you're looking for. Instead of standing over a paper with a red marker, you can simply type in a quality—age, religion, location, occupation, etc.—click send, and get back a semi-customized list of potentials. The things you need to be aware of before diving in are the number of members (remember, most of these sites are new), usability of the search mechanism, preservation of anonymity, ratio of men to women, member demographics, community involvement, and access to management.

To find out if a service is for you, try my simple test. Before you sign up at a new dating site, do a quick search of the existing profiles. Use the same criteria each time and record your results. After visiting five or six sites, you'll see the incredible range of results. If you interpret them as I'll explain in a minute, you'll know which one(s) is/are for you. (Yes, it's a bit like trying to decide which search engine to use when you're trying to find out some obscure bit of information—seems like it should be simple, but it's not.)

Part I

Start with this simple search to find out how many members there are in your age and geographic bracket, and the ratio of men to women.

> *Search # 1:*
> *Men seeking women*
> *Age range 30–45*
> *Location Pacific Northwest*
>
> *Search # 2:*
> *Women seeking men*
> *Age range 30–45*
> *Location Pacific Northwest*

Part II

It's time to make the search a bit more personal. Think about the following questions as you choose your search qualities:

- *Are you willing to be in a long-distance relationship, or do you want to date someone only in your locale?*
- *If you're looking in the Midwest, do you want your search narrowed down by state, city, or the entire Midwest?*

- *Do you have a choice of how to search location on this particular site?*
- *Do you want someone of your same age group? Older? Younger?*
- *Are you looking for someone of a particular race, ethnicity, or religion?*
- *Can you search by age group, ethnicity, or religion?*
- *Once you start searching, is it easy to refine or broaden your search, or do you have to start again, with all that waiting time?*

Now for the interpretation. The following are qualities that you'd want to see in an on-line dating service.

ENOUGH PROFILES TO BROWSE. A new site is fun to join, because every person who joins after you will see your profile. (A profile is a description of a man or woman who's joined the service, aka a detailed on-line personal ad.) But if there aren't many others on the site yet, everyone who joins will see *only* your profile. In terms of actually meeting someone on-line, it's not happening if there isn't choice. Choice is the main draw of the Internet, and combined with anonymity, it makes an ideal environment for picking and choosing potential mates. So head to the sites that have been around for a while. They offer you the most viable opportunities. Ideally, if you're in a metropolitan area, you'd want more than ten to twelve choices in your geographic area. If you're in a rural neighborhood, you'd want more than ten to twelve choices in your state.

GOOD SEARCH MECHANISM FOR BROWSING. Once you find a site where there are enough profiles, you have to make sure you can search them the way you'd like. For instance, some sites place more emphasis on proximity, others on giving you the largest possible choice in a wide physical area. Just like choosing a doctor or therapist, it takes time to find a search engine that you feel good about. By answering the questions in Part II of the test above, you're ready to analyze whether a particular search engine will give you the results you're looking for, be it divvied up by age, race, ethnicity, or location.

ANONYMOUS E-MAIL, HANDLE, OR SCREEN NAME. So if choice and anonymity make the Internet a popular place to meet other people, yet a matchmaking site doesn't provide anonymity, it's not worth much, is it? Most sites ask you to register with them, either for free or a small fee, at which point you choose an anonymous name to use while on the site. Once you start actively participating, you can send and receive e-mail from your new name, which is actually routed to and from your regular e-mail address. The key is that no one but you ever sees your e-mail address. You are the only one who decides if and when to disclose your real e-mail address to a potential suitor.

DECENT RATIO OF MEN TO WOMEN. Just like the rest of the Net, there are many more men than women surfing for dates and/or sex. Find a woman-friendly site, because if the ratio is greater than 2:1, guys don't stand a chance and women are deluged with responses. (While you may think this is a good thing, the truth is reading and responding to e-mails is hard work, and you don't want to be barraged by notes from incompatible people who are just responding because you're of the opposite gender.)

Now, try to remember fractions. If during Part I of the test above, your first search brought up eighty responses for men seeking women, and the second one gave you twenty responses, the ratio of men to women is 4:1. That's way too many available men—the ones who've joined this service are probably a bit desperate. Keep surfing!

AN AUDIENCE WITH A SIMILAR AGE RANGE, STATUS, IN-COME, ETC. TO YOURS. Take a quick look at the profiles. Are they all twenty-somethings searching for someone with whom to watch Beavis and Butthead? Are they mostly professional and older folks? Are they primarily computer geeks? Are most people on the service educated? Are they employed? As the old adage says, like tends to attract like, and a quick search should give you an idea of who's visiting any particular service. Think of newspaper personal ads—they have different qualities depending on the publication (i.e., *New York Magazine* or *Sunset* versus your local alternative newspaper). Be discriminating.

SINGLES COMMUNITY, IF YOU'RE INTERESTED. Some sites do more than just offer somewhere to place and browse ads. In fact, the trend is toward creating an on-line community—a place where singles can chat, post in forums (boards), get information—you know, hang out together. You have to decide whether this is an added attraction for you. On sites that do offer it, people who involve themselves in the community do infinitely better on the dating scene. They are minglers and tend to make lots of friends. And research has shown that couples who start off as friends, even virtual ones, tend to stay together the longest.

WAY TO CONTACT THE MANAGEMENT IF YOU NEED HELP. You want to be on a site where the shepherd is tending the flock. If there's no one to help you when you can't figure out the instructions, when your computer crashes for the umpteenth time, or when you're wondering about the "preying" qualities of a certain guy who keeps e-mailing you, you want easy access to the Web master. There should be a place labeled Contact Us, or Help, or an e-mail address visible from most pages on a site. It's called customer service.

Asking for help should be confidential—so feel free to speak your mind in an e-mail. The way you're most likely to get a positive response is to phrase your complaint as follows:

1) State that you really enjoy using the service because . . . (write one good thing about the site).
2) Let them know what date you used the service, what name you were using, and what process you were trying to perform.
3) Explain briefly what you found wrong or confusing.
4) Ask a specific question about how to make it easier

next time, or give a suggestion for how *you* think it could be simpler from your perspective.

5) Include your real e-mail address so it's easy for them to respond.

EASY-TO-DIGEST PHILOSOPHY OF THE SITE. Some sites are better known as dating palaces (where you'll find the same gals and guys who post personal ads in the paper and attend all the singles events in your town—aka professional daters). Some sites are better for finding long-term romance (where you'll find folks who are ready to commit). Others are best for quick-and-easy pickups (where you can find a date for a night when you're away on business or company for a lonely Saturday night). There's no way you can know which one's which unless someone spells it out for you. And that someone needs to be intimately involved in the management of the site.

Check out the philosophy of the service—often right on the introductory page. If you don't see a mission statement up front, see if there's a place to click called something like "About this service" or "Who we are." Read what they have to say about themselves, see if there are testimonials from people who've met on the service, and make a call as to whether they sound realistic. Send an e-mail to the Web master or site owner and see if you get a prompt, courteous, spell-checked response. Good intentions don't count—you need to know what you're getting into so you can get what you want out of the experience.

HOT ON-LINE DATING SPOTS

Webpersonals (http://www.webpersonals.com) is one of the easiest-to-use, free on-line dating services on the Net today. It works basically like the personal ads in the newspaper. You can either write an ad for yourself, or browse the ads already published. You are encouraged to do both. The motto on this site is, "True romance, a casual date, or an intimate encounter."

When you get to the site, your "click" choices include a search button, ask Amanda and Bruce (the relationship experts), create your identity (sounds like *The X-Files* to me!), success stories, and voice connection (a host of 900 numbers where you can meet others by phone).

Amanda and Bruce are straightforward, advice-giving people, but their credentials are not easy to find, so you can't be sure exactly who are behind their names. Moreover, in their very polite, rational answers, they often go beyond objective advice and tell people what to do. Their responses to questions like "How to avoid becoming a cyberjerk" are pretty harmless. But with more serious questions, like "I don't know if I should break up with this woman," their advice often seems based on scarce information from the user and without real counseling acumen. You may want to save your more serious questions for another site, and spend your time here reading Bruce and Amanda's more lighthearted answers.

Moving on to the search. You can browse the profiles without registering or creating a secret identity. But you cannot communicate with anyone on the site until you register. Once you do (a very simple process on this site), the administrator sends a confirmation to your e-mail address, you mail a reply back that you received it, and you're on your way to the virtual dating scene! The point of registering is to give you a secret name and password so you don't have to divulge your real name and e-mail address. This comes in handy when dealing with the weirdos; and it's easy to give up when you find someone you want to pursue.

One caveat about this site. It seemed like the pages took forever to download. Patience is a virtue, but when I'm seeing the same photos and icons over and over again, it gets old. Put on some good music or keep a book by your computer so you can stay occupied while you're waiting.

At Webpersonals, you can search by casual date, romance, or intimate encounter. Here's a sample of my experimental results of searches by romance:

Straight men, aged 35–45,
    living in San Francisco, CA   12 results
Straight men, aged 20–35,
    living in San Francisco, CA   12 results
Straight men, aged 35–45,
    living in California   175 results
Straight women, aged 30–43,
    living in San Francisco, CA   4 results
Straight women, aged 30–43,
    living in NY, NY   2 results

Straight men, aged 35–43,
> living in NY, NY   1 result (come on now!)

Straight men, aged 20–35,
> living in NY, NY   5 results

Truth be told, I was a bit disappointed, until I remembered that there are other ways you can search. Meaning, search by intimate encounter rather than romance. Oh, baby! It was all there. If you do the same search for straight men, aged 35–45, living in San Francisco, CA, under intimate encounters, the number triples to 35 results. There are fewer photographs (of the 12 romantic guys, more than a third had submitted photos)—are you surprised?

It turns out you really have to play around and explore in order to get the best selection of candidates for dating. There has to be something in between the 12 results you get from San Francisco and the 175 you get for all of California. Don't suggest Bay Area—you get another 2 results of straight men looking for romance, but they are not the same guys as the ones in San Francisco. Be creative in your search—don't stick with the obvious options. Most of the people in this database are highly educated (at least a master's degree) and earn a decent salary ($35,000 and up, up, yup!).

To create your own "identity," as Webpersonals calls it ("profile" as it's called on most other sites), you simply follow the directions. On this site, I created an identity for casual dating and answered an ad for romance. I received instant responses to both. I received approximately two to three new e-mails a day from men interested in dating. Their e-mails ranged from notes stating their vitals (I'm 5′10″, 210 lbs., brown hair) to those who really read my profile and reacted to it. Men say that when they post a profile, the response rate is more in the field of two to three a month. It's a woman's world out there—enjoy for a change!

As far as the ad for romance, the guy's first e-mail sounded decent. We exchanged flirtatious notes once a day or every other day. He gave me his phone number, and asked a few times for mine, but I wasn't ready to give that information out. A week later, the intrigue was over. We decided to stop using Webpersonals' anonymous e-mail and exchange our real e-mail addresses. His: I'mteninches@ degenerate.com. Even though he pleaded that it didn't mean anything, he lost my attention in less than the two seconds it took to read his screen name.

This started me thinking: I was responding to a romance identity, but since the site doesn't limit the number of identities you can have, it became clear that most guys have romance, dating, and intimate-encounter identities. So no matter which identity you see first and reply to, you'll most likely get the same answer—want to get together and have sex?

Check this one: Meet your mate by the stars at **Starmatch** (http://www.starmatch.com). This site provides you with astrological introductions, compatibility ratings, and relationship answers. Also available: your monthly horoscope, a members' chat room, store, and comments and testimonials. This is the newest thing to hit the Web.

Truly. It is so new there just aren't that many matches to be made in the heavens yet!

You have to become a member of Starmatch in order to browse or create a profile. In the member's agreement, the site states it is responsible for absolutely nothing. Period. (Must be in the stars.) To register as a member, you input information via the computer about the qualities of the person you'd like to meet (age, height, looks, body type, educational level, etc.). It's all on pull-down menus, meaning you don't have to type or learn how to spell, just choose from preselected options. Then you fill out a much more extensive form about yourself, including the above characteristics; your birth date, time, and place; hobbies; description of an ideal mate; how you spend your time; family values; and more.

You also have a number of choices in terms of how you'd like to be contacted by Starmatch, including phone, e-mail, e-mail only of those who match your description, e-mail only of those who match your description and are interested, etc. Starmatch does all the contacting, so you don't have to worry about your phone number going farther than the site's administrators. For the best results, check the widest variety of possibilities. For more prudent results, go for e-mail of those who match your description. Less wading through the muck this way, and less need to peel the leeches off your account later.

Once you complete the rigmarole, you get instant results about yourself and your compatibility rating based on astrological charting. It's very interesting—your attributes as based on the planets are rated as positive, somewhat positive, and challenging. Here are my results based on my birthdate and other info:

> *Congratulations for selecting STARMATCH. Your report features our Relationship Rating System, which is used to measure the compatibility between two people in the categories of Love, Friendship, Business, and Self-Harmony. The ratings are from 1–10, with -1 being the lowest score and 11 being the highest.*
>
> *Self-Harmony Report for Smart And Sassy*
> *Self-Harmony Index = 9.6*
> *Areas of Compatibility*
> **Sun Trine Mars**
> *The person who was born with the Sun trine Mars will probably be a powerhouse of energy and activity.*
> **Moon Conjunct Pluto**
> *Pluto is associated with spiritual energy or the divine essence of a human. The Moon's nearby presence will augment this basic energy. The individual might be a writer or teacher of spiritual ideas.*
> **Mercury Sextile Jupiter**
> *When Mercury, the planet associated with mental activity, is in harmony with Jupiter, this person will be skilled at expressing him or herself, and at bringing ideas out into the world.*

There are twenty total of these predictions about my personality and compatibility characteristics. I have five Areas of Potential Friction. You can also run these charts (right now for free) for you and a potential or current mate to see if you're compatible astrologically.

Once you've created a profile, you can head in and browse the others. Unfortunately, not only are there not that many at the time of this writing, but the ones there read like one big run-on sentence. Hopefully, they will get the kinks worked out with a little time (this site launched November 1997). After one week, I got one message from a person "who selected me." However, since I'm on the West Coast and he's in Iowa, I chose not to respond. When I clicked on "who I've selected," based on criteria in my profile, I came up empty. This site will make it or break it soon enough. As it's the only one of its kind on the Net and genuinely fun and interesting, I hope they're successful.

There are two more interesting matchmaking sites currently offering very large databases of members from which to choose. They also charge a monthly fee for becoming a member. These are **One & Only** (http://www.one-and-only.com/menu1.htm) and **Match.Com** (http://www.match.com). Both sites are similar in that they offer you just enough for free to entice you to pay the fee and become a full member. Very clever.

The motto for One & Only is "Sweaty palms, a racing heart, a quiver in the voice. That's what we're all about." For no charge, you can browse the profiles on this site, place an ad, and join a service that will contact you via e-mail if a new ad comes in that meets your criteria. What you can't do is answer an ad you find on the site. That costs $14.95 a month, $34.95 for three months, with discounted rates for longer periods. They accept American Express, Visa, MasterCard, etc. This site has a much more effective search mechanism than Webpersonals, so if you want to search for say, New York City AND the New York metropolitan area, it can handle it. A broad search on this site brings up hundreds of matches for your perusal.

Here are a few testimonials from the site (remember, these could have been written by staff, so take it all with a grain of salt):

> *I am a very shy, hard-to-get-to-know person. But thanks to One & Only personals, I have really gained self-confidence, and met a number of decent men. I have not had one bad experience. The man I am currently dating is nothing like I had asked for in my ad. He's older, 55, comes from a completely different background, doesn't smoke, and lives four hours away—much farther than I wanted to go to meet a man. In spite of all this, I agreed to meet him, after only a few letters. He has turned out to be the kindest, most romantic, fun, sensitive man I have ever had the pleasure of knowing. I am not sure how long this will last, I still have children at home, and he's ready to travel, but I will enjoy every moment, and have nothing but fond memories. Because of knowing him, I have learned to trust, to be more open, to strive for a better life for my children and myself. I know exactly what type of man I want in the future, if there is another man as wonderful as he is. Thank you.*

*I have been able to hit the jackpot through One &
Only personals. So very glad to have taken the first
step in meeting my Tennessee sweetheart through just
one simple ad. We have been writing since July, I have
traveled to Tennessee to meet her, she is visiting me in
California this Christmas, and all signs point to major life-changing events. Great experience with wonderful results.*

Match.Com (http://www.match.com) boasts that it's
"the most popular on-line singles community." I believe the
accolade is self-appointed, but what the heck? It *is* new media. This site is more comprehensive than some of the other
on-line dating services—it offers a complete community,
including relationship advice from Trish (a dating columnist who was the spokesperson for ISIS, the dating service
industry trade association), a monthly magazine called
MixnMatch, success stories, chat rooms, and a free seven-
day trial period. During the trial period, you receive all the
benefits of full membership—you can browse profiles,
place an ad, respond to ads, have fun! If you sign up to become a member before your free trial is over, it's only $9.95
the first month, and $12.95 each month thereafter. It does
get cheaper if you buy in chunks, i.e., buy membership for
a year and it's only $4.95 a month. But somehow, a year as a
member in an on-line matchmaking service doesn't inspire
confidence. They accept credit cards, checks, and money
orders.

The chat rooms on a Saturday afternoon on Match.Com

were relatively full—about thirty people. And the conversation was quite tame. Amazing. People were hanging out and talking. Nothing brilliant, but nothing smutty either. There is clearly a group of regular chatters on this site, which adds to the safety dimension of meeting people here. Tuesday nights there are scheduled chats with Trish, the relationship expert. (Remember, expert is not a professional degree. Visit the other sites mentioned in Chapter Three: Explore Your Sexual Self, and Chapter Five: Hot Monogamy, for licensed therapy and counseling.)

A quick search on the site came up with results of 2:1, men looking for women: women looking for men. Women can afford to be a bit selective, and they won't be as overwhelmed as on some of the other sites. You can search for members active in the last two months, one month, two weeks, two days, etc. This helps to make sure someone you contact is available and seriously seeking a partner. Most of the profiles in my search came up as professional folks, well educated, good writers, and looking for a relationship.

Last, here's a perfect example of the beauty of the Internet to preserve anonymity and help people meet others like themselves. **Selective Beginnings** (http://www. herpesworld.com) is a herpes dating service, offering herpes Internet personals from around the world. This site was created by a guy who "doesn't look forward to telling a would-be companion about his having herpes and who doesn't want to ask someone to take the risk of getting close to him." So people with herpes can partner with people with herpes. It's brilliant, and I can't think of any other way to get this community together anonymously other than in cyberspace. The Internet removes the stigma associated with having herpes by bringing folks in the same position together. Talk about a self-esteem booster; this is it. No more worries about when and if to tell a prospective date about your disease—you're all on equal turf.

There are currently 455 profiles listed in the United States on this site and a scattering more from other countries. It's fascinating, because in the profiles, there is no mention of herpes at all. People are comfortable in this safe environment, and they don't have to lie or apologize about their disease. The site has an anonymous e-mail system in place where you log in to a Web site to pick up your mail (it doesn't even come to your e-mail box—that's anonymity!). It also boasts a 900 line where you can call in and hear a message left by people signed on to the service. Ladies can call the 900 line free, regardless of location (sounds like wet T-shirt night at the bar to me!). It costs $10.00 a month to place an ad and receive an anonymous e-mail address. There's a three-month minimum; but on this site, it seems like a wise investment. Fees are payable in U.S. funds, check, or money order by mail.

VIRTUALLY COMPELLING

There's no doubt about it. Finding a mate on-line takes work, energy, and commitment. I have two friends who were noncommittal about writing their personal ads—one guy and one woman. So they decided that they'd each write the other's ad. While it was an interesting concept, it didn't work. First off, you know yourself best. Second, you need to infuse your personality into your ad. That's what makes these things work. Observe for yourself:

1) Hello. Are you someone special? I, like most computer professionals, am known to work long hours. But if you're attracted to these traits: easygoing, sincere, smart, funny on occasion, then I'm for you. If biking, movies, golf, good conversation, motorcycles, gardening, and love stories are some of your passions, then let's meet. If you're not afraid of trying new things, let's share some quiet moments together to get to know each other.

2) Hello there! I'm yet another computer engineer (not boring, I promise!). I've taken the college trip, done the work-hard thing, and I'm looking for that special life partner. I'm quite easygoing, well educated (PhD, but don't hold that against me!), kind, honest, sincere, a good conversationalist, and a good listener. In all modesty, I must admit that I've been told by women that I am physically attractive, so who am I to argue? But attraction is quite relative. Of course, having an "interesting" accent (I'm originally from South America), being a good dancer, and being in great shape doesn't hurt either! I'm looking for a woman who knows what she wants and how to achieve it, is honest, outgoing, intelligent, humorous, and attractive (to me). If men are intimidated by your intelligence and/or assertiveness, here's your

*chance to meet one who will not be. If you are seeking
a pen pal, an activity partner, or wish to explore other
possibilities if the chemistry is there, drop me a line; I
promise to reply.*

Okay, can you tell the difference? Both guys are probably
interesting, but #2 has a great personality. He writes in a
personal style that makes you want to keep on reading, instead of wondering what makes him so special. Note he
describes both himself and who he's looking for. Without
either one, it's only half an ad. And since you're not paying
by the word, it's good to include information about both
sides of the coin. You don't have to write an epic, but don't
sell yourself short either.

The only caveat is that sometimes people are good writers, but they forget this is supposed to be a nonfiction
exercise, if you know what I mean. So don't take anyone
at face value—if she's got a compelling profile, send an
e-mail and see if she can keep up the stream of clever
thought. If you continue to be impressed, you can move
into exchanging real e-mail addresses, then phone numbers (start with a work number, if at all possible), and see
if her abilities are text-only or if she can hold a two-sided
conversation also.

Here are a few key points from Delilah, **Thrive**'s resident sex and relationships expert, to remember when writing your on-line profile (http://www.lovehappens.com):

Make yours sing out. Check the profiles of folks who
are in the same age, gender, and professional

group as you. Then make yours different—make it stand out from the rest.

Follow example. Cruise through profiles of people you think you'd like to meet. See what qualities they're looking for. Then mention them in your own profile. Simple, huh?

Laughter is the great charmer. The people who are reading your profile—make them smile. Cleverness, intrigue, and wit are appealing. Nobody likes a downer (or a whiner or a crybaby), so keep it upbeat!

Be both positive and realistic. Focus on your strengths and accomplishments, making sure to embellish without exaggerating or making things up. No one likes to have their expectations raised only to be disappointed. Honesty up front is the key to a great relationship.

Get attention. Use your headline to tease and tempt. You've got very few words, so you have to be creative. It's easiest to write your profile first, then go back and either choose some words from it for the headline, or synopsize it into a snazzy, made-you-look one-liner.

Say what you mean. Have someone else read your finished profile to make sure there are no hidden meanings to your words. Another set of eyes before it goes public can never hurt.

First impressions count, so run a spell check. Proofread for grammar and typos. Remember, in this computer era, there's no excuse for spelling mistakes.

Smile through your words. Don't say you have a sense of humor—be funny. Don't tell people you're a hopeless romantic—be romantic. Be daring, be sweet—put your best self out there for the world to see. You'll have your choice of the lot—then you're in the driver's seat!

If you're still having trouble writing your profile after reading these tips, most sites offer profile consultation on-line. For instance, Match.Com has a profile specialist on site, who chooses one profile each month for a makeover. She posts it on-line and you have the opportunity to add your two cents. You can see the before and after profile and the subtle changes that really make it work. The specialist (who met her mate on Match.Com) writes a synopsis of how and why she made the changes she did, which is incredibly helpful when writing your own. Check out a few of the makeovers, and you'll get the idea.

Another possibility for ad-writing help lies at the **Relationship Center Online** (http://therelationshipcenter.com/top.shtml). The site offers a way to sign up for the relationship services offered at this Chicago center, including UltiMate Introduction service and referral services for psychotherapy. The UltiMate service is individually designed by you and can include comprehensive searches of up to 20,000 singles; psychological testing of potential dates; in-depth relationship consultation sessions, programs, and seminars; and personalized attention from Dr. Kate Wachs, a clinical psychologist specializing in relationship issues. Consultations last fifty minutes and cost upward of $125.00.

The other service offered at this site is personal ad consultation. Dr. Kate can write personal ads for you, choose the proper placement of the ads, and aid in screening and selecting the best responses. You do not have to live near Chicago for this service. Dr. Kate will be happy to schedule appointments by phone. She does not do consultations in private chat rooms.

PICKY, PICKY, PICKY

Don't answer every Tom, Dick, and Harry who writes to you. And for that matter, don't answer every Jane, Joan, and Sue. While there's something to the motto that there's no man (or woman) you couldn't date once, this is the on-line world and the numbers are much more intimidating than in real life. What I mean is, if you go to a dance and someone asks you out, you should give him your phone number and make a date. On-line, you will get so many responses for each profile you post (women more so than men), you really shouldn't feel obligated to answer each and every one. In other words, this is not the time to be "nice."

Trust your judgment. You took the time to read the advice and create a great profile. Did she? Or is she just trying to say what she thinks you want to hear? Is he just talking about himself, without any mind to your interests? It's important to keep up the banter for a while. Someone who responds to you in an automated way (Hi! I'm this height and weight and live in this place. I like xyz and I'm looking for abc. Give me a call.), doesn't deserve the time of day. This is work, and it's a two-way street. As a prelude to a healthy relationship, look for someone who's willing to share the burden and the fun, banter back and forth a bit, and be attentive to your needs while showing some of her own. Once you find this, you've got a winner.

Here's a range of responses to my ad that ran as follows:

SFBEAUTY   Looking for fun R&R in San Francisco

34-year-old female, located in SAN FRANCISCO, California, USA. I'm Caucasian (White). I'm 5′ 3″ with a slim body, I'm a social drinker. Are you interested in some scintillating evenings in San Francisco? Call me. I'm over-employed and need some fun R&R, no strings attached. My favorite restaurants are quiet and cozy with excellent food (must be better than I can cook at home!), movies are foreign films (although I won't say no to a good adventure flick), and world music (dance the night away . . .). Sound good? Let's go out.

1) Yes!
I'm Steve, 35, 6′ 4″, 225 lbs., with dark brown hair and green eyes. I like all types of music except country. I love rock and roll. I also like to dance, but haven't

*been in a long time. I've been divorced 5 years, have
no kids, and live close to you. Let me know what you
think. My e-mail address and phone # are below.*

The fact that he's been divorced five years is a turnoff. I
didn't need to know that piece of information yet. It's too
soon to know he's had one failed relationship that he's still
thinking about. Bye-bye, number one.

LESSON: Don't talk about your past relationships in your
e-mails, or even on the first date. Save it until there's some
trust built, and a context in which to put the information.
Otherwise you sound like you're stuck in the past and
haven't learned to move on. Don't unpack those bags in the
first e-mail.

*2) I've always enjoyed going out at night to San Fran-
cisco. I'm a Web master at an international company,
and work in the city. I'm 6 ft., in excellent shape (I
bodybuild), love movies, dancing, clubbing, and
restaurant experimenting. Wanna play?*

So, how are you different from everyone else? I know
you like to go out and that you have some money. I want to
know more about your personality before I'm willing to
spend time on you.

LESSON: Be very specific. "I love movies and restaurants"
could describe just about anyone in America these days.
(Does anyone cook anymore?) Tell the person why

you loved the last movie you saw. Describe your favorite restaurant meal and how you'd like to share it with the person you're responding to. Give your answer some personality!

3) I'm fun, humorous, love to laugh, honest, sincere, attractive. I'd love some R&R, movies, nice dinners, good food, dancing, music. I'm looking for friendship and possibly a long-term relationship.

I'm a single Asian Indian male, 5' 11", 32 years of age, black hair, brown eyes, athletic, fair, naturally tan, gorgeous looks, handsome, humorous, fun-loving, adjustable, simple, caring, sensitive, mature, honest, healthy, responsible, intelligent, ambitious, open-minded, positive, romantic.

I take good care of myself because I work to live **NOT** live to work! Most people find me a very interesting, funny, balanced person! I'm a very successful professional software consultant.

I am an active person and enjoy many activities: outdoors (camping, barbecues, volleyball, basketball), hiking, biking, movies, restaurants, playing tennis, going to the gym, dancing, live theater, sightseeing, walking on the beach, boating. Indoors I like listening to quality music (instrumental, classical, reggae), TV, reading, conversations and laughs with friends.

I have a photo profile (then he gives directions on how to get to it). *I'll admit the scanned photo didn't come out very good. I look a lot better in person as compared to the scanned photo.*

Talk to you soon.
(Two e-mail addresses listed and two phone numbers)

Geez Louise, is there anything this guy hasn't told me? I wouldn't know where to start if I were to write back. There'd be nothing to talk about because we've already been there, done that. With all those contact numbers, you'd think he was desperate or something.

LESSON: Keep a little mystery in the equation. If you tell all in the first e-mail, there's no reason for anyone to reply. Ask questions. Give just enough information so someone else wants to ask questions about you, too. You don't want to overwhelm, but entice.

4) Hi,
Would you consider meeting a European guy? I'm Danish, 36, tall, dark blond hair, slender, and attractive.

I moved here to the Bay Area from Europe two years ago and I work as a senior sales engineer for a small software company. I like computers, but I'm no geek. . . . Interests? Many . . . Actually too many for the time I have available. I like cooking European food, movies, music of almost any kind, exploring the Bay Area, weekend escapes, lazy Sundays, travel, and lots of other things. I speak several languages—but I'm still considering learning one more. . . . Just haven't decided which one yet. My favorite movies these days are "The Full Monty" and "Secrets and Lies." Naturally I like foreign movies, some of them are not that foreign to me :-)

I am looking for friendship and fun. Interested or curious? Then drop me a line and we'll see what happens. Hope to hear from you.

This guy comes the closest to making it happen. He gives some specifics about what he likes (note his favorite movies these days). He has some personality—"I like computers, but I'm no geek," and he's an explorer—"I speak several languages—but I'm still considering learning one more."

LESSON: Be yourself. Infuse your personality into the e-mail rather than expecting the words to tell your story. But you already know this by now.

ADVICE FOR THE CYBER-LOVELORN

Negotiating cyberrelationships can be tricky. So can real-life ones, but most of us have a bit more experience with them, as well as a support system of friends who understand. The rules for cyberromance are developing as we speak. And the truth is, all's fair in love and war.

But you've heard all about the dangers of cyberromance—meeting people who could be mass murderers, for god's sake! Don't be naïve. Entering into any kind of relationship can be dangerous if you're not "street-smart." Go in with your eyes open, and your sensors on, and the Internet can offer a plethora of new, great people to meet.

Here are some tips for moving an on-line flirtation to a real-life encounter. While none of them are foolproof, if you turn up empty-handed in a number of these explorations, you'd better start wondering if this guy's been telling you the truth.

- Check the person's name and address in the phone book. Is she listed? Does she live where she says she does? Is she listed under a man's name?
- Make sure that not only does he call you, but you call him, both at home and work. Just a simple check of the phone numbers AND to see who answers the phone (i.e., if he says he's a big exec, it had better be a secretary picking up his line the first time, not him answering the phone for a big exec).
- As you're talking over the Net, poke around to see if you have any friends in common. If you do, call and see what opinions you get.
- If she says she loves a certain restaurant, or frequents a neighborhood bar, head on over. Take a photo of

her with you, and ask the service staff for a character reference. Sounds crazy—but they say a person who treats staff generously is a winner.

- Ask your new friend for references. Then call them. One from work, one family member, and one good friend. Hear what different people have to say; and listen for the unspoken messages.

- Meet the first time in a public place. If you feel more secure, ask a friend to come along and wait at the bar. If that seems excessive, make sure at least one person knows where you are and when you expect to be home.

- Don't hesitate to let the wait- or bar staff know that you're meeting a guy for the first time. They will naturally watch out for you.

If you're looking for current on-line tips, a few sites offer solely cyberlove advice, but most have "agony aunts" (or uncles) who will address both on-line and off-line relationship issues. (See Chapter Three: Explore Your Sexual Self for some good columnists.) If you're serious about finding love on-line, you might check out the **CyberLove** site (http://hem.passagen.se/offend/). This site is the home of two people who met on-line and offer constructive advice and peer support to help people define the "rules" of cyberrelationships.

And a few testimonials from folks who have successfully met on-line, so you have some impetus to follow through on all you've learned in this chapter:

Yes, wedding is the end result but let me tell you about the beginning. October 96 was the start of my computer Internet experience. I placed an ad in the pen-friends section of an on-line service. I love writing, so was hoping to get a few replies. Lo and behold, over 900 replies came to my e-mail box. During the first week of replies I sifted through 200 or so responses and decided to write to about 10 people who sounded interesting. (There were a lot of weirdos replying, so be careful!)

One of the replies came from a guy called Walt from Texas. I thought he sounded fun and I really enjoyed corresponding with him. We both eventually installed chat programs onto our computers so that along with e-mails we could chat as well.

As the months passed telephone calls began to creep in as well as flowers, music tapes, letters, and photos. I eventually began corresponding with Walt only, giving up my other penfriends. I was going on holiday to Europe and Mexico the next month (I live in Argentina), and together Walt and I decided we could meet up during this time as Texas is not that far from Mexico.

Anyway, I flew into Texas to meet him. He was there waiting at the airport gate. I recognized him instantly from the photos. We moved closer and gave each other a warm embrace—it felt like there was no one else on the earth but the two of us. After a few minutes we felt as if we had known each other for years.

We spent 3 days exploring Texas and getting to know each other on a more personal level, before flying off on a whirlwind holiday in Mexico. It was on the second-to-last day that the marriage proposal came. . . . It felt like it was meant to be that we had been thrown together.

We feel that we were two souls in the world who had been separated and we have now come back to-gether. Walt is my friend, lover, soul mate, and future husband.

CONCLUSION

True love is possible, no matter the venue for finding it! And when you're in a small town, or shy, or too busy to get out much, the Internet offers a safe, dynamic place to meet po-tential mates. As long as you can balance your wariness with your willingness to be open, you can have a great time out there. And trust your instincts—if you feel yourself "going love-blind," call a friend and have her keep you in check before you raise your expectations unrealistically and live to regret it.

Speaking of diving in, how about sex? You meet some-one, and you know you really like each other . . . when does sex enter the picture? How do you discuss safer sex with a new partner? Even if you've been with the same person for a time, don't you have burning sex questions floating around in your head because you don't know who to ask?

The Internet saves the day. With an abundance of sex educators, counselors, and therapists available to answer your questions in chat rooms, forums, and advice columns, you'll never again be left wondering how to make your partner ecstatic. Read on to the next chapter, "Explore Your Sexual Self," so you'll know where to find the best sex ed around.

ANNOTATED SITE LISTINGS

http://www.webpersonals.com Webpersonals is one of the easiest-to-use, free on-line dating services on the Net today.

http://www.starmatch.com Starmatch provides you with astrological introductions, compatibility ratings, and relationship answers.

http://www.one-and-only.com/menu1.htm One & Only currently offers a very large database of members, and charges a monthly fee for service.

http://www.match.com Similar to One & Only, Match.Com offers a large database that you pay a monthly access fee to search.

http://www.herpesworld.com Selective Beginnings is a herpes dating service, offering herpes Internet personals from around the world.

http://www.lovehappens.com Delilah, Thrive's
   resident sex and relationships expert, offers tips
   to remember when writing your on-line profile.
http://therelationshipcenter.com/top.shtml
   Relationship Center Online offers personal ad
   consultation by Dr. Kate Wachs.
http://hem.passagen.se/offend/ Advice and support
   on the CyberLove site from a couple who met
   on-line.

EXPLORE YOUR SEXUAL SELF

We've got sex all around us these days, but tell me, how much do you really know about the subject? With beautiful, sexy women selling perfume and gorgeous, half-naked men pimping jeans, we're barraged daily with steamy TV prime-time moments. But when was the last time you saw two people (other than yourself and a partner) engaging in intercourse until they're spent? You never see an embarrassing moment in the media either—a guy who loses his erection, a woman who can't lubricate enough, or a couple who falls off the bed while in the throes of passion.

Sexy is public. Sex is private. We're left in a lurch. A society obsessed with sex, we have no clue about what's normal in terms of bedroom experience. Unless you're the type who buys those how-to manuals, or one of the rare folks who talks to your friends and family about sex in an open way, you're left wondering: Am I normal? Am I doing this right? Am I a good lover?

It's hard to know where to start getting sex information that's more advanced than what you got in high school. You may try to bring up the subject in conversation with a friend, your doctor, or a therapist. And the response? It's "that look"—you know, the glare that says, "You're having sex? If it's true, I don't want to hear about it." Or you get the silent, knowing nod. Either way, you're left wondering.

The computer boom of the nineties is the best thing that's ever happened to sex. We finally have a place to learn the more advanced techniques and find out how we each measure up to the rest of the world. The anonymity of the medium, the lack of shame and embarrassment, and the accessibility of sexual health professionals is sure to change our lives forever.

In this chapter, I'll show you how to find:

- The best sites for sex information and advice
- Real-time chats with sex experts
- One-on-one virtual sex therapy
- Peer forums for open discussion of sexuality

But first, here are some facts about human sexuality. This way, we'll all start on the same page:

- The average man lasts three to five minutes from the beginning of vigorous thrusting during intercourse until ejaculation.

- The average penis is five and a half to seven inches long when erect (the smaller, flaccid penises grow more to reach full erection).
- All women have a G-spot, but it is only sensitive for some.
- Men have an analogous organ to the G-spot called the prostate. For many men, stimulation of the prostate just before ejaculation can intensify orgasm.
- Some women emit a fluid when they orgasm, similar to a male ejaculation. But not all women can do this; it's a biological function women are born with or without.
- Most women need direct stimulation of their clitoris in order to reach orgasm. With clitoral stimulation, many women are capable of multiple orgasms.
- Men need a refractory, or resting, period after ejaculation. As men age, the refractory period gets steadily longer.

Okay, that's enough. Time to sign on.

VIRTUAL INFORMATION AND ADVICE

The Internet is the perfect place to get the right answers to all your sex questions. Think of it as a virtual library of sex, and plan on spending some time searching for information on a topic you've always wanted to know about. Instead of doing an all-out search on the Web, if you go to a few select sites you'll be able to find what you're looking for fairly easily. Information on premature ejaculation, women who can't orgasm, contraception, and penis size abounds. The beauty of these sites is that it's easy to find what you're looking for, and much, much more. It's inevitable that you'll get distracted reading about sexual possibilities you didn't even know existed! And you'll most likely learn something as you click away.

Sexual Health

One place where sex information is available in an easy-to-digest fashion is the **Sexual Health Info Center** (http://www.sexhealth.org/infocenter/). You can search topics like Better Sex, Safer Sex, Aging & Sexuality, Sexual Dysfunction, and more. Wondering what you get when you click on the Better Sex button? A new set of choices—love and toys, vaginal sex, anal sex, oral sex, and positions. When you click on love and toys, you have to make one more choice (well, which toys do you want to know about?) before you can delve into the actual information. If you go down the vibrator road, you'll have questions answered such as What is a vibrator? What's the difference between a vibrator and a dildo? Why would you want to use a vibrator? and What to look for when you buy a vibrator. The information in each category is well written, thorough, and easy to read. Here's a sample:

> *What is the difference between a vibrator and a dildo? You may not have guessed it, but vibrators are not primarily used for vaginal penetration. If you*

thought they were, you might have been thinking about dildos, which are most often used for penetration. Vibrators are quivering, electric devices that come in all shapes and sizes, and are used most often on the exterior of a woman's genitals for sexual stimulation. They can sometimes resemble the male sexual organ, but the most popular brands and styles do not represent any human body part whatsoever. Women can use vibrators to stimulate their clitoris, vulva, vagina, and anus. Men can use vibrators to stimulate their penis and anus. Couples can use vibrators together to enhance the pleasure of sexual intimacy.

Sexuality Library

One of the most extensive virtual libraries of sex information is housed in the **Society for Human Sexuality at the University of Washington** (http://www.sexuality.org/ ftpsite.html). Everything you ever wanted to know is right here; you just have to weed through it. Two caveats about this site: There is no search mechanism, so you have to scan the entire index to find what you want, and the information provided is not guaranteed. The site is a true library—all information is cataloged and available for your perusing and borrowing pleasure, but you have to decide for yourself which reading is worthwhile. You can find interviews, reviews, and topically arranged articles on subjects ranging from G-spot stimulation to nudism to sexual political activism. Read at your own risk—some of the articles are amazing, others are nasty drivel.

Sex Advice

On the other hand, a site known for its quality sex information is **Thrive@Passion** (http://www.thriveonline.com/passion.html). Here you'll find selections from well-known books about sexuality like *Contraceptive Technology* (Hatcher, et al.) and *The New Male Sexuality* (Zilbergeld). You can review STD rates in the United States, the risks associated with oral sex, the art of Tantra, and more. But the highlight of this site is the advice from Delilah, the resident sex and relationships expert.

It's time to change "person" here. I'm Delilah, and I've been answering questions on the Internet for five years, first as Alice of the **Go Ask Alice!** site at Columbia University (http://www.goaskalice.columbia.edu/index.html) and now as Delilah@Thrive. I've answered over 750 questions as Alice and 300 more as Delilah to date (1/98), on topics ranging from contraceptive options to healthy amounts of masturbation to handling the green-eyed monster of jealousy. I give no-nonsense, reliable, mature answers to your questions about sex and relationships. They're fun, nonjudgmental—even witty at times. Half a million people visit the Delilah area each month, and the number is constantly growing.

What have I gleaned from answering your sex questions

all these years? Well, first, most of you have the same questions. Second, most of your questions about sex are pretty basic—you want to know if what you do in the bedroom is the same as everyone else. And more often than not, it is. (Although there are always a small number of you who dive off the deep end with topics like bestiality!)

I get hundreds and hundreds of questions each day. And every weekday I choose one to answer based on its human-interest appeal and educational value. While one of you writes a question to me, hundreds of thousands of you read the answer. Don't worry, though, all names and identifying information are stripped from the questions before they're posted on-line.

To give you an idea of the scope of questions, here's one of my favorites:

Dear Delilah,
Remember "When Harry Met Sally"? And the scene where Sally faked an orgasm in the diner? How do I know if my wife's faking it in bed or not?
—Suspicious

Dear Suspicious,
There is such an emphasis on orgasm during sex that many men believe if their partner doesn't have an orgasm, the sex wasn't good. In fact, some men think they have to generate not one but multiple orgasms for their partner each time they have sex. And the orgasms have to be quick and loud, so the men can feel good knowing they've satisfied their partner.

Physiologically, it is not only easier for men to orgasm—it takes much less time. It takes women longer to lubricate, engorge, and release. Often by that time, their partner's asleep. In order to make their men rest easy, many women do fake those quick, noisy orgasms that guys seem to want.

So, how do you know if your wife's faking it or not? Ask her! Now, don't ask her while she's in the throes of passion or just after you've made love. Ask her at a neutral time, when you both are feeling relaxed and good about the relationship. Ask her if she's ever felt pressured to fake an orgasm. If she says yes, ask her about the circumstances surrounding it. This is a great opportunity for you to find out what she likes in bed and to let her know if there's anything you'd like done differently, too.

In a nutshell, use your wondering to start a dialogue with your wife. Although the first words may be difficult, there's a good chance your sex life will improve significantly from the discussion.
Love,
Delilah

Before you consider asking Delilah a question, use the excellent search mechanism on the page to see if she's answered it before. For example, a search for the word *masturbation* turned up 118 results, including the following choices (my comments in italics):

- All about masturbation *(why would you need more?)*
- Too much masturbation? *(how much is too much?)*
- Addicted to masturbation? *(it IS possible)*
- Breakfast cereals and masturbation *(don't you know about Mr. Kellogg of cornflakes fame?)*
- Never had an orgasm *(this is definitely a woman . . .)*
- Dirty magazines *(common masturbatory tool)*
- Women who can't reach orgasm with their partners *(not as unusual as it sounds)*
- No erections with new woman *(can he get erections during masturbation?)*
- Men want it more *(masturbation's a viable option!)*

There are many different ways of approaching the same subject, so a search is a great way to start exploring Delilah's world. Go Ask Alice operated on basically the same principle, except it covered more territory—sexuality, health, nutrition, etc. Alice was a bit more serious than Delilah, and the content was geared toward college-student issues (safer sex, condoms tearing, relationship breakups). Delilah's crowd is a bit older and more worldly. However, the Go Ask Alice site was a pioneer in terms of providing sex information on the Internet. Started in 1992 as a text-only computer service for Columbia students, by the end of the year, the material was translated into html, the programming language of the Web. By 1995, when the World Wide Web became common knowledge, Alice had already answered 770 questions.

Here's one of my favorites. It is also one of the first questions I answered in my Alice alter ego:

Alice—
I have a question. Was it common for people who
grew up in the early 50s, relatively "square" people
such as my parents, to engage in oral sex? Sorry, but I
just can't picture it. I also seem to remember that it
was considered something of a taboo.
—Me

Dear Me,
Your question reminds Alice of an article entitled "Is
There Sex After Forty?" by O. Pocs, et al., which is
based on research about whether or not college stu-
dents thought their parents had sex and how fre-
quently. It concluded that for the most part, college
students could not picture their parents having sex.
The students' assumption is that they "did it" as
many times as the number of children they had, using
a procreative model as their rationale.

According to Kinsey, adults in the 1940s did have oral
sex. Not all adults, but some. The incidence increased
based on educational level—60% of college-educated
couples engaged in oral sex, 20% of high school edu-
cated couples, and 11% of grade school-educated
couples in 1948. Remember, too, oral sex is, and was,
a form of contraception. In addition, it is an intimate
way to give and receive pleasure. Funny to see parents
in that role, isn't it?
—Alice

It's been a pleasure to be answering your sex and relationship questions over the years. I've learned so much about human nature, and hopefully I've also helped you by making sex information more commonplace and accessible through the Internet.

Safer Sex

While you're out there surfing, don't forget about safer sex. The Durex-brand condom homepage (http://www.durex.com) is just one of many sites that cover the topic. This lively site has a clinic nurse dispensing accurate information on sexually transmitted diseases and how to use a condom. There is also Dr. Dilemma, who can answer all your safer sex questions. To top it off, you can read about the history of condoms, how condoms are made, and partake in a confidential global sex survey.

Dr. Ruth

Two more sites worth mentioning are **Dr. Ruth's Sexually Speaking** (yes, that's our very own Dr. Ruth Westheimer) on ParentTime (http://pathfinder.com/ParentTime/dr_ruth/homepage/ruth.home.html), and **Internet Sex Radio** (http://www.radiosex.com). Both sites use RealAudio technology—cool software that lets you listen to a radio talk show while Web surfing. If you don't have the software installed on your computer, once you get to either of these sites, you'll be prompted to click on the RealAudio link at http://www.realaudio.com where you'll find directions on how to proceed. (Remember, if things get complicated, click on the Help button and read the instructions. This experience is worth plugging along to the finish.)

Okay, now that you're geared up, here's what you'll find on these two sites. Dr. Ruth does weekly sex therapy sessions with parents. Every week, there's a new problem, ranging from whether to lock the bedroom door, to a wife's anger about not getting enough sex, to a man's fear about having sex with his pregnant wife. You use the RealAudio player to hear Dr. Ruth's intro to the week's session. Her comments are right on target and unforgiving. She delves into the heart of the issue in ten seconds or less, as only Dr. Ruth can. After hearing her comments, you read the transcript of the session itself. Then you can register your vote in an on-line poll as to how you and your spouse deal with the issue at hand. Here's an example. This couple has two children, ages five and six.

DR. RUTH: *What seems to be the problem?*
EDDIE: *My wife's a nudist.*
MICHELLE: *I am not! I would never walk around naked in front of strangers.*
EDDIE: *But she doesn't care if the kids see her naked.*
MICHELLE: *They're not strangers, they're my kids.*
EDDIE: *It would be better if they were strangers.*
DR. RUTH: *So your objection to Michelle's nudity is the effect it might have on the children?*
MICHELLE: *They could care less. They've been seeing me naked all their lives.*
EDDIE: *How do you know what it's doing to them?*

The damage might not show up until they're teenagers.
MICHELLE: *And maybe not being so hung up will help them develop healthy attitudes about sexuality that will last for the rest of their lives.*

POLL: Do you let your children see you naked?
Yes, we're very casual about nudity.   *25%*
It's OK if they see us getting out of the shower,
but basically we keep our clothes on.   *46%*
No, we make sure our children never
see us naked.   *29%*

Surprised? If you want to know about other parents' sexual practices, peruse the archives of Ruth's goods—they are arranged chronologically, and are easy to pore through. Dr. Ruth also answers four questions each week for parents, such as Why is it hard to be romantic when there's a baby in the house; My thirteen-year-old is masturbating; My husband's spending too much time on the computer; Sex after a C-section; and more.

Internet Sex Radio

The other site of note that uses RealAudio technology in a more extensive way is **Internet SexRadio.** Hosted by a Canadian sexual health expert, the segments are equivalent to radio call-in shows. Users are invited to send in questions via e-mail and the hosts answer them in the weekly hour-long show. The shows are recorded, then made available on the site for download anytime. You can surf the Web or do other computer work while you're listening. The shows themselves are a bit slow-moving (probably very slow-moving on a 14.4 modem), and suffer from a lack of strong personality. I imagine more of these weekly radio segments will crop up, and in time, we'll have our own Internet sex shock jocks!

CHAT WITH THOSE IN THE KNOW

There *is* a way to get instant answers to your burning sex questions without researching an on-line library, listening to an hour-long broadcast, or checking an advice column to see if your question has been selected. A few sites offer real-time chat with sex experts and professionals. These sites strive hard to maintain a sense of order and politeness in the rooms. This is no easy task, given the helter-skelter environment on the Net and the way some people inevitably get when they hear the subject is sex. (It's true. For some inexplicable reason, full-fledged adults start acting like teenagers when they talk about sex.) But with skilled chat hosts and sexuality professionals, a number of sites manage to provide a mature environment so you can get your sex questions answered in a hurry.

The downside to these sites is that you have to wait your turn. If you're not first in line, you have to listen to everyone else's problems first. This can sometimes be an asset, as often someone else has the same question as you, and asks it first. Then you're off the hook! Speaking of off the hook, these are public chat rooms, so you do have to ask your question in front of other people. While sex therapists and counselors operate under the belief that there are no stupid questions and take each query as a learning opportunity, some of your fellow chat mates may not be as open-minded. You might have to withstand the scrutiny and heckling of other chatters. This type of behavior stems from ignorance, and if you can get past any taunting, chat rooms staffed with professionals are still a good place to get advice.

When you're surfing, look for sites that have a licensed sex therapist, educator, or counselor working the rooms. You can tell if there's a seasoned professional by reading the bio of the chat host or expert, which should be easily accessible from the homepage of a qualified site. Here's the drill:

1) You click on a site, read the bio of the expert, and you're intrigued—she or he seems like someone you can trust.

2) You click a bit more, and get to the point of having to download software. (On some sites, you can click on a button that says Chat and the software will automatically appear, compatible with your browser (skip to #4).

3) You either give up or plod on, hoping your computer doesn't crash from the new software.

4) You get the software loaded. You now have to register and create a chat name. Don't use your professional name to go into the chat rooms. You may get

deluged with junk e-mail afterward; it's too easy to identify you in real life; your coworker could be in the room that night; and if you're a woman and use your first name, you'll get instantly "hit on." Instead, choose a lighthearted name without any double meaning—something like I'mCurious, or OpenEyes or StarryNight.

5) Head into the chat room with your new name.

6) Look for instructions as to the protocol for the room. Read them. If there are no instructions, say hello and sit in the room for a while to watch the train of conversation.

7) Some hosted rooms have a system in place whereby questions are taken in turn and the professional or expert answers them. Other rooms have a topic of discussion for the night, and encourage everyone to join in.

8) Take a deep breath, and jump into the fray.

Dr. Patty Britton is one of the most well-known sex therapists on the Web. She was the creator of The Sex Clinic, and ran very successful nightly chats on the site. Now you can find her answering questions on **The Women's Network** (http://www.ivillage.com/content/0,1625,1258,00.html).

One evening I visited the chat room on the former Sex Clinic site and found nine people plus Dr. Britton chatting. Subjects included premature ejaculation, women's orgasms during intercourse, control during sex, masturbation, and foreplay. Here's part of the conversation that ensued:

GUEST1: *My boyfriend doesn't last long at all. Once he starts pumping, he has to stop moving pretty immediately or else he comes.*

GUEST2: *That happens to me, too. It feels so good to be inside my girlfriend that it's hard not to come. But if I stop moving, it's bad because it breaks the mood.*

DRB: *Younger men tend to get overly excited and pop too fast. Older men may be losing their erections. There are basically four reasons why men suffer from premature ejaculation: 1) You get overexcited. 2) You haven't learned your own sexual pattern. 3) You're afraid of something—like she doesn't love you—and you lose it. 4) You have bad training from masturbating and coming too fast. Getting over premature ejaculation involves retraining yourself. It's up to the guy, and the guy alone, to change his pattern.*

GUEST3: *I'd really like to last ten minutes or more.*

DRB: *I'd have to check the stats, but any man can last longer, as much as an hour if he learns to manage his responses.*

GUEST3: *One hour?!?!?!*

DRB: *There's a great book by a famous sexologist, William Hartman, called "Any Man Can." Dr. Keesling also has good books on staying power in sex for men. It's all about learning to control yourself and being the patient partner to assist the process.*

GUEST4: *My husband doesn't believe women can have orgasms with intercourse.*

DRB: *Over three-quarters of all women do not have*

orgasms with intercourse. The rest do, and all can learn. For many women, foreplay is the main event.

GUEST5: *If more people got involved in foreplay, there'd be better sex overall.*

GUEST6: *Only way a man can be sure to pleasure a woman is through foreplay, oral sex.*

DRB: *Not for all women, and not for all men, Guest6. But that is the general consensus.*

GUEST4: *It's gotten so that I don't want to have intercourse anymore.*

DRB: *For some folks, sex is more about intimacy than mechanics. Guest4, maybe you and I need to have a one-on-one in a private room to discuss this in more detail.*

(Read on in the chapter for information about how this works.)

GUEST5: *Bottom line is to make sure that each partner is satisfied.*

DRB: *Right.*

GUEST6: *Guest2, have you tried to gain more self-control through masturbation?*

DRB: *Here's the kicker: You are responsible for your own orgasm, erection, ejaculation, pleasure, not your partner. Accept that responsibility, don't rely on your partner to get you there. If you're not satisfied, do something—say you're not happy with the sex, change the pattern, or leave.*

GUEST2: *Yes, I can last a long time during masturbation by slowing, increasing, different speeds, etc.*

DRB: *Guest2 and Guest6 are onto something. Masturbation is the foundation for all sexual experiences. Get it down here and you'll have a better sexual time with a lover.*

DRB: *I get the feeling that you go with the flow, Guest2, that you follow her controls, and derive your pleasure from what she doles out to you. And because you're not expressing your real passion, you pop quickly.*

GUEST6: *It's not only important that she's satisfied, but you as well.*

DRB: *Right, Guest6. Guest2, you are stuck on her, not your own needs and pleasure. If you made that shift, sex would be different. Could you try to refocus yourself for a week?*

GUEST2: *Since we only have sex three times a month, that won't work.*

DRB: *How about trying for a month, then?*

On America Online, you can find excellent sex education and advice on the **Thrive** site (Keyword: @Passion). The Sexuality Salon offers professionally moderated chats on sexuality and relationships nightly. The room holds forty-eight people, and each chat lasts for an hour. Experts range from yours truly, Delilah, the resident sex and relationships expert; to Dr. Bernie Zilbergeld, author of *The New Male Sexuality*.

On most nights there are thirty to forty people in the

Salon, and the environment is calm and interesting. When you enter the Salon during a scheduled chat time, you'll receive an "instant message" (a small pop-up box on your screen) that describes the chat and the procedure for joining in.

Each scheduled chat is a question-and-answer session with one of a mix of male and female experts who are PhDs, social workers, and therapists. If you have a question for the expert, you type a question mark and then wait until one of the moderators calls on you in turn. When you're called on, you type in your question and the professional will answer it. It's that easy! You wait your turn, then get your time. And it's much cheaper than seeing a private sex therapist—it's free!

Here's a brief excerpt from a chat with Bob Berkowitz, author of *Male Sexual Fantasies*:

GUEST1: Why do men like to fantasize about being with two women?

THRVBob: Great question, Guest1. It is men's number-one fantasy for several reasons.

1) It appeals to the visual senses. It's no secret that men are visually stimulated. . . .

2) It also relieves men of the pressure of having to satisfy a woman.

3) It may, for some men, relieve them of any obligations of intimacy.

4) Finally, two is better than one!

One warning, guys. Sometimes your wife or girlfriend can develop a crush on the other woman!

GUEST3: Oh, please, one can be just as good. ;)
That's why some fantasies should remain just that—
a fantasy.
GUEST5: I agree, fantasies are the BEST.
GUEST2: That's true.

What are the most commonly asked questions in the on-line chat rooms? From my experience facilitating two chats a week for two years now, I'd make the following list:

- How much masturbation is too much?
- My penis is (anywhere from eight to fourteen inches) long. Is that normal?
- My partner doesn't want sex as much as I do. What can I do?
- My wife won't perform oral sex on me. How can I get her to do it?
- I want to try anal sex. Is it safe? How do you do it?
- How can I drive a woman (or man) wild in bed?
- My sex life is getting boring. How can I spice it up?
- I have no sex life with my wife/husband anymore. I'm thinking about having an affair with a person I met on-line.
- I think my partner is cheating. What should I do?

Of course, you'll have to visit a chat room yourself to find out the answers.

UP CLOSE AND PERSONAL

If there's not a sex therapist in your neighborhood or you're afraid everyone will know if you make an appointment, you can get personalized therapy anytime at two reputable on-line sites. You send in your sex question via e-mail to a licensed professional, and for a fee you get a private response. Most problems can be answered in an e-mail message, but there are options for more complex situations. In these cases, you can sign up on-line for a phone, in-person, or virtual therapy session, with a fee comparable to about half that of traditional therapy in a major metropolitan area.

The pros: You get personalized responses from a respected professional. You don't have to wait, mess around with other people's problems, or have anyone else know you're asking for advice. The downside: You have to pay for information and advice you can find elsewhere for free. If these therapists can answer your question in one e-mail, I'd venture a guess that with a small amount of time and effort, you can find what you need on any of the sites listed in this book. E-mails are useful as a tool to help you decide whether you like the therapist's style and depth of knowledge. If you do, you've found someone you can trust to do some deeper therapeutic work. If you don't, you've spent less money shopping for a therapist than if you met in person.

One site where you can get individualized, virtual sex therapy is called **Sex Therapy Online** (http://sexology.org/). "Dedicated to providing the on-line community with the leading information and advice regarding human sexuality," this site is operated by sexologist P. Sandor Gardos, PhD. He is a licensed clinical psychologist, and a fellow of the American Academy of Clinical Sexologists and the American Board of Sexology. Sex Therapy Online is not a substitute for face-to-face therapy and may not be appropriate for everyone.

On the site, you can get private e-mail consultation from a professional sex therapist at a cost of $25.00 per question. The answers average 1,000 words in length and are either written by Dr. Gardos himself or a respected colleague.

You can also schedule a phone, Internet, or in-person consultation with a sex therapist at this site. You fill out a form with basic information about yourself and the nature of your question or problem, and you're contacted within seventy-two hours to discuss fees, type of appointment, and potential times to "meet." On-line appointments are held in a private chat room and are a good option if you don't have the privacy for a phone conversation. At a cost of $80.00 for a one-hour session via phone or Internet, it's about half of the going rate for in-person sex therapy— $150.00 an hour.

In the introductory e-mail, Dr. Gardos encourages you to schedule a phone consultation rather than an on-line one, because he feels more can be said in a limited amount of time. He also suggests an e-mail consultation to begin with, as it's less expensive and can be quite effective in situations where in-depth therapy is not required. You can always switch to another form of therapy later if the need arises. Here's an excerpt from an on-line consultation with Dr. Gardos, reprinted with permission of the client, so you get the idea of what this is like. This "session" took place in a private chat room, and lasted over an hour. The client was conflicted by feelings of being attracted to many men, while at the same time wanting only to be with her loving fiancé.

> *DRGARDOS: Okay, let's talk about your partner for a sec. What is it that makes him unattractive to you now that wasn't true earlier in the relationship?*
> *CLIENT: He used to be more commanding, mysterious in bed, and I think even physically I used to be more attracted to his looks, his scent, his everything.*
> *DRGARDOS: I am struck by your use of the word "mysterious." There is a word: limerance. It refers to that initial rush you feel when you first meet someone you are attracted to. Some people get very "addicted" (for lack of a better word) to that feeling. There are ways to enhance a (long-term) sexual relationship, and recapture some of the magic, but again, it *will* be different . . . better in some ways, but different.*

I can only imagine that more of these on-line therapists will start springing up, if it's determined to be a lucrative business. For the therapist, it's much simpler than running a full-time office and seeing people in person. The benefit to you is professional counseling while maintaining your anonymity—important when dealing with sexual situations or if you live in a small town or community. Since most sex therapists are located in the major U.S. metropolitan centers, the Internet provides an extended network of professional help and advice for all your sexual problems.

If you'd rather find a sex therapist in person, but don't know where to start (the Yellow Pages doesn't always have an obvious category), you can try the **American Board of Sexology** site (http://www.sexologist.org) to find a sex therapist in your area.

TALK IT UP!

For peer sex information and advice, head to the bulletin boards and on-line forums. They're unmoderated (I've yet to find one that is truly, diligently maintained by a sex therapist or educator), so leave plenty of time to sort through the assortment of posts. Some messages are going to be clear; others will leave out the details. You can post a message yourself and get excellent advice or the ramblings of a lunatic. It's catch as catch can, and some people like it that way.

You need to register on each site to post a message, but not if you just want to read what others have written. If you find a site you like, it's worthwhile to register, because there's sure to be something to spur you to react, if not start a new topic. A trick when you register—check to see which items are mandatory to fill out on the form. Most often, it's simply a screen name and password and you're off. However, many sites will ask for much more personal identifying information on the same form; look closely, usually they have a tag saying optional. Fill out the minimum, as you may end up with piles of unsolicited e-mail in your box once you start handing out your vitals.

Boards are organized by subject, within which are messages and responses. Messages are identified with a subject line, like "Where's my wife's G-spot?" Responses are labeled "Re: Where's my wife's G-spot?" Topics, messages, and responses are not always arranged as you might expect, so click on a number of messages to find a strand of conversation you find interesting.

Some sites have developed communities and sophisticated discussions. Most of the sites I've mentioned in this chapter have bulletin board systems in place, so if you're checking them out for other info, the boards are worth a look-see. There's also an interesting, diverse community at **Bianca's Smut Shack** (http://www.bianca.com). (Don't mind the name—it's got shock value and that's about it.) One of the older Internet communities, Bianca's site is set up as if it's her house, with various rooms where you can go to chat and post on the boards. Some of the rooms tend to be more risqué (for example, the bedroom is wilder than the parlor, as you might expect). It costs $10.00 to become a member of Bianca's community for six months, $100.00 forever. And it's worth it, because it's no holds barred in the Smut Shack.

The major topics on boards in all of the sexuality sites are as follows, with sample postings of what you could expect to find under the headings:

- orgasms
- body image

I've been overweight for years, and very conscious of how I look. Regardless, I've never worried about having those pesky lights on during sex. I figure if a man finds you sexy and attractive with your clothes on, they just plain find you sexy and attractive—end of story. The lovers I've had have never complained about my looks. Rather they've commented on what they particularly love. Whether that's having a lush, welcoming body, sensuality plus, and a real passion for lovemaking, or personality, intelligence, and humor—once a man's attracted to you, just accept it and appreciate what you have in front—or under, or on top of, or behind you! Life's too short, this is NOT a dress rehearsal!

- G-spot
- premature ejaculation
- relationships
- oral and anal sex

I am truly in need of some help. I have the most wonderful boyfriend, but due to negative experiences in my past, I am unable to do what he really desires— give him a blow job. I am so afraid I will not do it right or that he will be bored, so many negative thoughts run through my head. Any suggestions? I really need all the help I can get; I want to surprise him with this very special treat.

Answers ran the gamut from intellectual, soft-porn descriptions of oral sex, to the less profound, as follows:

In Reply to: *Help in the oral sex department*
Be open with him, have him show u what 2 do and tell u what he likes and dislikes. Say things like:
"Hey do u like this?"
"No . . . try this . . ."
"U mean this?"
"YEAH!"

- affairs
- sexual desire
- fantasies
- shaving
- breast size/penis size

I am 23 years old and my girlfriend and I are in love. The only problem is that I am not confident of my penis size (14.5 cm erect). Every time we're making love, I start thinking about it and sometimes I get so upset I lose my erection. I am afraid that she isn't satisfied and would prefer that I had a larger one. I've been obsessed with this since I was 16. I am so afraid she's disappointed with my size. What should I do?

Re: Small Penis
Don't get caught by the fallacious-phallus urban legend. Being a sensitive, attentive, caring, and informed lover is far more important than penis size; and good lovers don't measure. Your size is of concern to you only. Communication between partners is the key to good sex, not genital size.

One of the caveats of the boards and forums is that they each use different software, so it takes some time to figure out how the messages are categorized. Some are listed by subject; some are chronological with most recent or oldest first; some are considered "threaded," meaning sorted by theme, others are free-for-all; some show you ten messages at a time, some bare all the contents at once. Most people find a board that suits them, and continue posting there. It's easier this way because you don't have to learn too many sets of rules. Also, you can get to know the other posters, build community, and provide some continuity to your forum visits.

CONCLUSION

I've covered most of the major existing sex education and counseling sites out there at the time of this writing. More will be cropping up as sex educators realize what a valuable medium this is for reaching and teaching people. Whether you're reading an advice column, chatting with a sex expert, or on a message board learning from your peers, the bliss of privacy in getting your sex ed on the Net is not to be rivaled.

One form of sexual expression we haven't yet explored is fantasies. Most men and women have them; they can be visually explicit or fleeting glimpses, but they are the heart of the sexual spark. In this chapter, you found out where you can ask the sex questions that you have now; in the next chapter, "Fantasy and Desire," I'll show you how to take things one step further in the fantasy world of cybersex. From anonymous sex to role-playing and scenes, you can turn on more than your computer when you surf the Net.

ANNOTATED SITE LISTING

http://www.sexhealth.org/infocenter/ The Sexual Health Info Center provides comprehensive sex information on most major topics.

http://www.sexuality.org/ftpsite.html The Society for Human Sexuality homepage contains an extensive virtual library of sex information.

http://www.thriveonline.com/passion.html Thrive@Passion provides quality sex information including book excerpts and the Ask Delilah column.

http://www.goaskalice.columbia.edu/index.html Go Ask Alice is a health question-and-answer service for college students.

http://www.durex.com The Durex brand homepage

contains comprehensive information about safer
sex in the '90s.

**http://pathfinder.com/ParentTime/dr_ruth/
homepage/ruth.home.html** Dr. Ruth's sex advice
for parents at ParentTime.

http://www.radiosex.com Internet Sex Radio uses
RealAudio technology to provide virtual talk
shows about sexuality.

**http://www.ivillage.com/content/
0,1625,1258,00.html** Dr. Patty Britton provides
consultations to help you with your sex
problems.

http://sexology.org/ Sex Therapy Online provides
e-mail, Internet, and phone fee-for-service
consultations with a professional sex therapist.

http://www.sexologist.org The American Board of
Sexology site helps you to find a sex therapist in
your area.

http://www.bianca.com Bianca's Smut Shack has a
well-developed on-line message board
community discussing issues of sexuality.

CHAPTER FOUR

FANTASY AND DESIRE

Cybersex can be a wonderful experience. It is the coming together of two minds—joined for the pleasure of mind-sex. (Of course, if done right, it can be VERY physically rewarding as well.) You describe your actions instead of doing them. Each partner tells the other(s) what you're doing, what you want to do, and how you feel. Using your imagination, you can set scenes that enhance the activities or otherwise play a role in your experience.

If you remove procreation from sex, what you've got left is fantasy and desire, not to mention physical pleasure. I would venture a guess, though, that the driving force behind sex in the 1990s, whether you're partnered or single, is the human imagination. Whatever we dream about, hear about, fantasize about, sex is never quite as good as what we imagine in our minds. So we use our desire and our dreams to spur us on to the next sexual experience.

Imagination is boundless. But as human beings, we're prone to forget that simple fact. Many of us find some form of erotic stimulation during puberty or young adulthood, then stick with it for a lifetime. We get lazy, or we don't know where to look for other ideas, or we simply become creatures of habit—knowing the motions that turn us on and using them regularly.

Enter the world of cybersex. The place where imaginations go wild, anonymity is the rule, and desire runs amok. The place where experimentation is commonplace and routine is frowned upon. As Robin Hamman in his M.A. dissertation writes, "The loss of inhibition on-line allows (people's) on-line selves to take part in sexual activities without violating any moral stance they may have in real life."

For cybersex to be interesting, it has to emulate reality. But you also have to be able to do something in the virtual that you can't do in the real. That's the key.

Cybersex has to be similar to real life, but take things one step further. Consider this—in real life, you can only remember one partner with whom you had great sex. Enter cybersex, where you can turn on your computer and experience great sex with many people virtually.

In this chapter, I'll teach you:

- What cybersex is and where to find it
- Why people do it
- How to use cybersex to enhance your real-life sex

But before you sign on and get started, I want you to think about what it is you desire sexually. Following is a list of different things to get you thinking in the right direction. Check off the ones that you might like to explore. Choose things that you've never done with anyone, but you've occasionally (or frequently!) dreamed about, or read about somewhere. Fantasize away (it's only an exercise!).

___ More partners
___ Deeper intimacy with one partner
___ A sexy partner
___ To make love with others watching
___ To watch others make love
___ To have sex with someone of the same gender
___ To attempt something slightly "kinky," like anal sex or using sex toys or role-playing a scene with a partner
___ To initiate making love with a partner
___ Power and control play
___ Casual sex
___ To experience being desired
___ To make love with more than one person at a time
___ To masturbate with another person
___ To learn how to talk dirty
___ To explore your sexual fantasies
___ To feel what it's like to "watch" someone get aroused
___ To become more comfortable with your body and your sexuality

___ To have a sexual experience without cheating on your partner or losing your virginity

___ To enjoy safe, disease-free sex

If you're uncomfortable checking off activities from this list, try the following exercise to stimulate your desire:

Begin masturbating alone, then stop once you notice your body changing—men becoming erect and producing "love drops," women's vaginal lips swelling and beginning to lubricate. Instead of taking yourself all the way to orgasm, stop and focus on your thoughts. Are you thinking of your partner? A potential partner? Someone attractive you saw on the street one day? A place? A feeling? What exactly is it that is arousing your desire at this moment? (Women, if you haven't masturbated, or have yet to experience an orgasm, I highly recommend a book called *For Yourself*, by Lonnie Barbach. An inexpensive paperback, this book is well worth every dollar.)

Focusing on your thoughts and feelings as you become aroused will help to put you in touch with your sexual desires. Then you should be ready to go back and see what you might like to choose from on the sexual activity list. Checking off an item doesn't mean that you'll ever do it. The idea is to start thinking about the range of sexual expression and expand your sexual comfort zone before we head into the nitty-gritty of cybersex, where, if you so desire, you can realize your fantasies virtually.

The Definitions

Sexual fantasies. While it may seem obvious what they are, sometimes it's not so black-and-white. Fantasies are thoughts and images you have in your mind, things you dream about that stay in your mind and heart without being realized. Men and women who use fantasy as a sexual tool and a path to arousal are often the most sexually active folks around. They find the greatest number of different sexual experiences appealing, and are generally comfortable with their sexuality. Fantasies keep imagination alive and your sex life sizzling.

Some people have been able to use their sexual fantasies as a creative turn-on with a partner. They tell each other their innermost secrets and imaginings, and use it to propel a sexual experience. Other people use fantasy as a tool when they are without a partner, to get through the lonely nights or as a sort of practice session—imagining what they might do if they had a lover.

Problems arise when people confuse fantasy with desire. That is, when they feel they have to live out their fantasies. Fantasies are best as they are—kept in your mind. Often when people try to realize their fantasies, things sour quickly. Jealousy, fear, or discomfort keeps one or the other person(s) involved from feeling satisfied by the experience. But fantasy used to fuel desire? That's a great thing. Fantasy as a method to arousal, fantasy as a substitute when you're single, as practice for real life . . . they all work. And since the Internet is the brave new world of the imagination, what better place to play and experiment?

WHAT IS IT?

All this talk, but what exactly *is* cybersex? Cybersex comes in many different forms, all of which are computer-mediated tools to become aroused. Here are some of the ways people currently engage in cybersex:

- People take turns typing instructions and descriptions of what they are doing to the other person and to themselves on the computer screen while masturbating in real time. This is usually done in private chat with two or more people.
- Many people participate in the writing of interactive erotic stories on-line with the intent of arousal. Of course, reading them can be quite arousing, too.
- Some people engage in virtual sex—remember Woody Allen's Orgasmatron in the movie *Sleeper*? Today there really is such a thing as computer simulation of sex. The technology has not quite caught up to the imagination though, so don't expect much more than you'd get in a theater with 3-D glasses when the movie's shown in slow motion.
- There is software available where men can create

their own virtual girlfriend. This software was developed in Japan and is said to be misogynist; it's not widely available in the United States.

I'll focus on the first two, most common forms of cybersex. Before I get ahead of myself, here's an example of a typical cybersex exchange where two people meet in a chat room on-line and then head off privately to take turns typing sexual instructions and descriptions to each other. The two protagonists are Joe and BettySays.

> *<Joe> What does Betty say?*
> *<BettySays> Betty says she's gotta have it.*
> *<Joe> Do you deserve it?*
> *<BettySays> I've been a good girl.*
> *<Joe> You're gonna have to prove yourself.*
> *<BettySays> I'm a beautiful woman. My breasts are perfect, and my body is shapely. I'm petite, with long brown hair and big blue eyes.*
> *<BettySays> I would like you to take care of me. . . . Tell me what you'd to do to me.*
> *<Joe> Where are you right now? At your desk? What are you wearing?*
> *<BettySays> I'm at a glass table. I'm wearing a black teddy under my day clothes—jeans and a t-shirt. All black.*
> *<Joe> Take your pants off and unsnap your teddy.*
> *<BettySays> Okay, hang on two secs, lover. I have to close the curtains.*

<BettySays> My pants are on the floor, strewn.

<BettySays> My teddy is unsnapped, exposing myself to the world.

<Joe> Sit back down. Put your feet up on the table.

<BettySays> I'm sitting at my glass table, looking down at myself through it.

<Joe> Put your feet up. Spread your legs wide apart.

<BettySays> I'm at my chair with my feet on the table, open wide.

<Joe> Now take your hands and run them down your thighs.

<Joe> Don't touch your button yet. Just get your hands by that lovely crease at the top of your legs.

<BettySays> I love that spot, too.

<Joe> Now take your fingers and lightly spread your lips. Show it to me. Is it wet?

<BettySays> Do you like what you see? I'm wide open.

The story gets juicier, as you might imagine. BettySays starts talking less and less, as Joe describes what he's doing to her. Once Betty is fulfilled (noted by "ohhhs" and "aaaaahhhs" typed to the screen), they switch and she takes the lead typing, describing, and instructing Joe to his climax.

In some ways, this form of cybersex is the same as reading erotica, except two people take part in it. It's also similar to phone sex, except it's more anonymous because you can't hear another person's voice or heavy breathing. Like other forms of erotic stimulation, all you know about the person you're cybering with is whatever he chooses to tell you. And since the whole thing is about fantasy, you can tell each other absolutely anything.

> *There's something amazingly hot about knowing I'm turning somebody on so much that they orgasm. And about doing it myself while I "listen" to them.*

Here's an example of the second type of cybersex—the typing of interactive stories with the intent of arousal. The following was posted on a public bulletin board, and was written by three different people:

> *#1: You're tied down securely, with silk ropes of course, and all mine to do with as I please. I glide my body slowly, sensuously, up the entire length of yours, making sure my hard nipples rub against your chest and face. You can feel how wet I get as I cup my breasts with my hands, bend forward, and rub your lips with my nipples . . . first one, then the other. I demand that you take them into your mouth, pressing them together and offering both at the same time.*
>
> *You want me on your face, don't you? I move up until I'm straddling your head, one of my thighs on each side of your face, my sex directly in front of you, enticing you. You can smell my scent. You know how hot I am now, and you know how hot I can get. My sex is above you, but just far enough away that you can't reach it, no matter how hard you strain and try. My hand slides down my body, caressing, until I reach the*

113

wet folds. I run my middle finger lightly along the center, barely opening the lips. You would like your tongue there, wouldn't you? I spread my lips open wide with one hand and start stroking my button with the other.

Do you like watching me play with myself? I'm gonna make myself climax soon. I rub harder and faster. I can feel your body twisting and jerking, trying to break free. Finally, you lie still. You're watching my hand work its magic.

I can't stand it any longer, I've held it off as long as I can. I let out a scream. I move down and take your hardness in my hand and guide it to my mouth. I'm still shaking from my orgasm and I want you to join me. My mouth slides up and down, sucking with each stroke. I switch to my hand, stroking you . . . faster and faster, until you explode. Your body jerks in spasms of ecstasy, until the only sounds that can be heard are the pounding of our hearts and the sounds of ragged breathing as we collapse . . . exhausted, satisfied.

#2: I was unsure of this being-tied-up business, but I wanted you and you insisted, so the lady gets what the lady wants. I felt the tension in my wrists and my body as I tried to take you. My mind was captivated, too. Seeing you lying there glowing, a small smile on

your lips, awakened a rawness in me, a deep urge. It was "THE BEAST." Your eyes locked onto mine, sensing the emotion. I moved toward you, keeping your eyes locked. I growled low and deep, saying "I AM TIGERMAN, I WANT PUSSYCAT." You whimpered as my voice reverberated off the walls. I told you in a low growl to move in front of me and spread your legs. Seeing your pinkness, your full lips, I growled my pleasure. You let out a whimper. You were looking at my erection.

I prepared to drink from you as I would a stream. I leaned forward and licked you firmly. You cried out. I lapped your juices, licking you clean. You were shaking, trying to hold my head in place. I growled, and moved toward your pretty button. I used my tongue to press firmly against your button as you continued to writhe . . . little orgasms, wave after wave.

#3: Mmmmmm . . . good stories, people. They make my panties all wet and hot. I sit here rubbing myself with two fingers in small circles as I read. I'm at the edge of my chair. My legs jerk slightly as I rub faster and harder. I can feel myself getting hotter and wetter. I tighten instantly around my fingers and feel the pulsating contractions. My breathing is low and fast. I move my body back and forth along my fingers . . . faster and faster . . . back and forth as I throb pleasurably. . . .

What's different about this form of cybersex—the interactive storytelling—is that you can enter the fray at any time. It doesn't take place in real time, as the typing and describing do. Many more people can take part in it—anyone can jump in and tell part of the story whenever they like. Sometimes these stories continue over a period of months; other times they fizzle out quickly. When you get a few good writers involved, the story line can get incredibly steamy. In fact, some of the best writers have gone on to develop their own e-zines and newsletters on-line.

The interactive storytelling is a safe place for complete freedom of sexual expression. Anyone can write anything—they can tell their deepest fantasies or share their best real-life lovemaking experiences. The thrill comes from both the writing and the reading, as well as the anticipation built up between episodes: Who will write the next chapter? Will a new character emerge? Will there be betrayal, loneliness, or intrigue?

The other secret to this type of cybersex is that there are many more people reading the stories than writing them. Meaning that millions of people participate in these stories as voyeurs, simply reading them to expand their sexual horizons, and if they desire, to get turned on. The anonymity, the creativity, and the easy access to the material make this form of cybersex quite popular.

Interactive erotica can also take place privately in e-mail. Two people may get together after becoming intrigued with each other's writing styles in a forum, on a message board, or in a chat room and begin a one-on-one correspondence. This can be very exciting as the stories are then tailor-made to the two people, more so as they get to know each other's likes and desires.

Any chapter about cybersex would be remiss if it did not mention the danger of addiction. This book is entirely focused on using the computer as a tool to enhance your real-life sex life, so my advice will always be to sign on, experiment with cybersex, then turn off your computer and decide how to use your newfound knowledge to turn on in your real life. It's important to remember that many of the people you will meet on-line are already addicted. They spend hours every day and night on-line, meeting people for cybersex. They are dreamers, living in a fantasy world, who have not yet figured out how to make the leap from the on-line world into the real one. While they may have charming personalities on-line, they may be socially inept in person. You will definitely notice these folks if you frequent a particular chat room, as they tend to find a community and stay there. Often they are the hosts of a room, greeting the "regulars" and charming the newcomers. Your job is to keep your cool and remember what you're doing on your trips into the world of cybersex. It can be an incredible tool if you use it responsibly.

WHY DO IT?

I've alluded to the many reasons people engage in cybersex. Here I'll lay out the driving forces as follows:

- desire
- exploration
- anticipation
- anonymity
- control

DESIRE. The most common reason people engage in cybersex is to experience the feeling of intrigue and passion that occurs in the beginning of a romantic relationship. In real life, it's not unusual to get sidetracked with daily chores and responsibilities. These can lead to your taking your partner (if you have one) for granted. If you don't have a partner, the distractions keep you from meeting anyone new and experiencing the high of new love. Cybersex can provide an outlet—a way to feel loved and desired by another person, seemingly without imposing on your real-life relationships and responsibilities.

> *I loved hearing she loved me, that she couldn't wait to be with me. . . . She reminded me of my early relationship with my wife when things were not hampered by bills, problems at school, and leaky faucets.*

The debate is raging as to whether cybersex is considered cheating. Most women say yes, most men say no. These are both broad generalizations at best. No matter what you think, the key is to use cybersex as a tool—take your reawakened desire off the computer and into your real life. While it sounds tricky, it's actually possible. It takes sincere effort and hard work, but it can be very rewarding. If you don't move your feelings of desire to your primary relationship or use the energy to find a new relationship, you end up spending too much time in a fantasy world and cultivating a destructive coping strategy—escapism.

How do you move desire from the computer screen to your real life? Think of what the guy said in the beginning of this section: The cybersex relationship reminded him of his marriage in its early days. That's exactly what you have to do—if you're in a long-term relationship, bring back the feeling of desire that existed in the very beginning. How do you do that? Remind yourself of what it was about your partner that first attracted you to her. What is it about your on-line relationships that attracts you to various people? Compare and appreciate—appreciate your partner for her qualities, remember why you desired her in the first place. Sometimes it's as simple as reminding your partner that you think she is hot, and hearing that she feels the same way. Get sexy with abandon, just like you do on-line with your cyberpartners. Remember, if you don't use it, you lose it!

> One night I stumbled into a chat room named something like hot spot, hot place, hot something. I loved it there! I was the only girl in a roomful of guys. They were all vying for my attention. What a way to stroke a girl's ego.

Really! How often does it happen that you feel desired by a whole group of members of the opposite sex at the same time? For women, you have to have large breasts, or an amazing figure, or be wearing some really sexy clothing. And then the attention you get is only because of that trait. For men, you have to be incredibly handsome or sexy, or an exotic dancer at a bachelorette party. You get the idea. Most of us rarely get positive attention just because we exist— enough attention so that you feel desired and loved. The on-line world can provide a temporary feeling of self-esteem and worth. If you learn how to appreciate the feeling and bring it into your daily life, cybersex can become a valuable confidence-building tool.

To do this, you have to bridge the gap in your mind. If these people can love you without even knowing you, then why shouldn't other people who know you love you? People who know you are more aware of your positive qualities, giving them all the more reason to want to be around you and make you feel loved. Your job is to remember what your good qualities are and learn how to project them in your daily life and, of course, with potential dates. So you don't have large breasts or a fat wallet. That's okay. You have a quiet wit and you're great with words. You know it because you've charmed people in the chat rooms with your talents. There's the catch—you've met people, made new friends, even had lovers—without relying on any of your physical traits. Bring your nonphysical qualities to the surface and you'll shine in the real world. Use the Internet and the chat rooms to build your confidence, to learn what desire feels like, so you can re-create it in your day-to-day interactions. With your newfound confidence, you can get out there and meet more people, hoping to hook up with the man or woman of your dreams sooner rather than later.

I was chatting with a man one night and we just started talking about what we were wearing. He asked for a picture of me, so I sent him my most recent glamour shot, and he got off on it. I was excited to know that my looks could make a man so turned on.

Okay, now we've taken desire one step beyond anonymity. The exchange of photos—sexy photos, nude photos, "glam" photos—is a very common part of cybersex. While not all are willing to engage in the exchange (for safety reasons, as well as not having the self-confidence necessary to take, no less send, a sexy photograph of oneself), as this woman attests, it can be a great turn-on. Sometimes called gifs or pics, photos can enhance the visual stimulation in cybersex. And many of us enjoy the visuals.

Sharing of pics on-line can be a great way to boost your ego on a physical note. It can be frustrating to always see pictures of perfect-looking, scantily clad women and men in magazines and on TV. By exchanging amateur photos, we're changing the way we've been taught to get aroused. The pictures aren't perfect, and neither are the bodies, but they are still sexy. As the woman above realized—you're flattered when an anonymous partner finds you attractive enough to become aroused. The process reminds you that you're a sexual being; it awakens the sexuality that's been dormant in many of us for too long. It can help you become more comfortable (and less ashamed and guilty) about your body and your living, breathing sensuality.

EXPLORATION. Cybersex gives you the time and the space to try new things. Think about it: Have you ever talked dirty to a partner? Have you considered it, but you're just too embarrassed to try? That's the case for most of us. According to the Janus Report on Sexual Behavior, by the early 1990s, American men and women were about equally accepting of talking dirty during sex (58 percent of men and 57 percent of women agreed it was either "normal" or "all right").

One of the biggest turn-ons to talking dirty is simply breaking the social taboos of niceties. People who talk dirty say the ruder, crasser, and naughtier the words are, the better the turn-on. Feeling it's normal, or that you'd like to venture into the world of the forbidden, doesn't mean you give yourself permission to do it. When you start counting how many people actually participate in sexy verbal seduction, it's a much smaller percentage.

I love my wife but she is reserved in many respects. She wouldn't say "shit" if she had a mouthful. Cybersex gives me an opportunity to talk with women who are less inhibited than my wife. I've been married 37 years and have no intention of changing that. But I believe the cybersex has improved our sex life because I have become more adventurous, and am teaching her how to loosen up, too.

There are so many times we are influenced by our partners, and even potential partners. If you think someone close to you wouldn't like you to talk dirty because he is more shy about sexual things, then you don't even consider doing it, even if you know it would turn you on. In the scenario described above, the man realized he was missing out on an activity he enjoys, so he engaged in cybersex with "less inhibited" women than his wife. The beauty is that he brought it all home; since he was more comfortable with the act of talking dirty after doing it in cyberspace for a while, he was able to be more relaxed in discussing it with his wife, and teaching her what he likes. Not too shabby . . .

The same thing happens when you share your fantasies during cybersex. While you may have always felt fearful about telling a partner your sexual fantasies, once you break the silence during cybersex, you can become much more open in your imagination and with your partner.

> *Since my husband can't type, I do it for him when he's*
> *on-line. His first cyber experience was a blast for both*
> *of us. We had a great time on-line and an even better*
> *time afterward.*

This couple has completely integrated their fantasy cyber life with their real-life relationship. And for the next couple, what began as a private fantasy became the impetus for more intimacy in their marriage.

> *When I started getting involved with cybersex, I was*
> *embarrassed to have my husband read the things I*
> *wrote. Now I make sure he knows everything. Trust is*

a part of marriage. And our sex life is even better because of it!

If you're close enough with your partner, cybersex can be an effective tool to use together, or to use alone to set the stage for real-life sexual excitement later. Cybersex is also a great way to explore your own sexuality. In the next chapter, I'll tell you about various sites where you can read and learn about the most common forms of "kinky sex." But in cybersex, you get the chance to try it out—to practice in writing, with a virtual partner—and see if what you think might turn you on really does. Many people who engage in cybersex say they do things on-line that they had never even considered in real life.

During cybersex one gets to experience erotica as it's being written by someone who can tailor the story to your sexual preferences. Many of us have never been with anyone who says or does the sexy, exciting things we crave. Cybersex allows us to retreat into our imaginations and experience some of the wild sexual adventures we don't dare do in real life.

With cybersex, you can let your fantasies run wild. I've done things in cyberspace that I would never have done with someone in real life.

Simply the act of becoming more comfortable with your sexuality via cybersex can lead to better real-life sex, not to mention the expanded sexual repertoire you get from listening to the folks with whom you're cybering. Letting your imagination run wild can be an incredibly liberating experience. It teaches you that all the inhibitions and taboos we have around sex are self-imposed and that shame is a useless emotion. Living in the moment, enjoying your experiences, reveling in your sexuality—it's something we're not taught to do, and cybersex is a great way to learn as adults. It will naturally spill over into your real-life sex life—just be careful not to get too caught up in the fantasy of it all. The key to enjoying cybersex is being able to bridge the gap between virtual and real, to use the experiences to enhance your sexuality and self-esteem. Getting caught in a fantasy world is no fun for anyone . . . and it's self-destructive in the long run. The key to exploring on-line is remembering to turn off your computer and enjoy life.

Getting back to exploring, masturbation is the best way to learn what you like sexually, and to teach a partner how you like it. While some engage in masturbation during cybersex and some don't, most do. And masturbation is healthy—it's a good tension release, and helps you become more comfortable with your body. Cybersex is just another stimulation to help you get there.

You can make important discoveries about your own body during cybersex. With this knowledge, you can begin to really enjoy lovemaking. Think of this self-discovery in the same way you would a new book of culinary secrets.

Cybersex starts with learning about your own body. While men are generally more comfortable touching themselves (most boys start masturbating naturally in prepubescence), they can still learn a lot from descriptions of how new people tell them to masturbate. I know this is a stretch for many straight guys, but gay men are the best people from whom hetero men can learn. Gay men both have the equipment themselves, and spend their lovemaking time pleasuring other men. Hanging out in some of the gay chat rooms can be eye-opening for heterosexual men who are not threatened by the idea. Chatting in a gay room does not mean a man is gay—it means he's wise enough to know who to learn tips and tricks from about his own body. Just another way to expand your horizons in the safe, secure environment of cyberspace. (On the Web, you might try **Planet Out** (http://www.planetout.com) or on **AOL**, Keyword: OnQ. Both are mature, responsible, hip sites for exploration.)

For women, comfort with their bodies has never come quite as naturally as for men. Learning how to masturbate was either something we were lucky enough to stumble upon, or a thing some open person along the way taught us to do. Engaging in cybersex is a way to relax into your body—learn how to touch it in new, pleasurable ways; learn how another person might touch your body if given the opportunity. So many women say that simply the experience of masturbating with another person, albeit anonymous and virtual, has given them the courage to explore their sexuality, not to mention find new areas of pleasure and sensations they hadn't even considered.

ANTICIPATION. Sometimes it's not the event of cybersex itself, but the buildup that is so incredibly exciting. One of the problems with having sex with the same person for a long time, or even having sex with many partners in the same way over the years, is the lack of anticipation and mystery. By sharing cybersex with one person in e-mails or publicly in the interactive bulletin boards, you can stoke your imagination. You can revive "the thrill" of passionate beginnings, as you wait to check your e-mail box for a new love note, or sign on to check the new chapter in an erotic story. You can use this desire and anticipation to stoke the fire of your love life—whether partnered or single, it doesn't matter. The excitement spills over effortlessly. You walk around with a smile on your face, knowing you have something to look forward to, and people will react positively. Your sensuality is awakened.

> *I had no experience with cybersex, and in fact my ad said just that. And now I had a virtual woman living in my mind and memory . . . a very, VERY pleasant feeling. Our e-mail was once a day, or at the most, two. Starting the computer was an event in itself . . . expectation . . . anticipation . . . excitement . . . the thrill of seeing "that" e-mail in my box.*

ANONYMITY. The anonymity of cyberspace allows a sexual freedom that is rare in our real lives. It allows us to have casual sex without fear of disease or pregnancy (remember the 1960s!), to stretch our social codes of what's "normal" sexually, to overcome physical challenges, not to mention it affords a new way of engaging your feelings with someone with whom you're having sex.

Think about it. In real life, it's impossible to have casual sex these days without a discussion. It's the 1990s and we've got sexually transmitted diseases, including AIDS, to consider. But also, casual sex is not hip. It seems like everyone has to talk about everything, discuss all the possible issues in their entirety before getting to know someone intimately. It's like the sexual revolution of the 1960s never happened; it's hard to find someone to have a safe, fun, sexual encounter with anymore. Women become emotionally involved, and men feel responsible and obligated. One-night stands are a thing of the past. Except in cyberspace.

> *The cool thing about it* [cybersex] *is you never have to talk to the other person again if you don't want to. It's a lot harder to do that IRL* [in real life]*!*

In addition, the anonymity shakes off all preconceptions based on physical appearance or dexterity. You can continue to have an active sex life on-line after life-threatening surgery, if you're physically challenged, or if you're experiencing a sexual dysfunction. You can still be appealing to the opposite sex if you're verbally dexterous.

> *I think cybersex is a great option. We are ALL sexual creatures, sex is not BAD or DIRTY, it's natural, passionate, and fun! As for the fact that you could be talking to anyone when you are cybering, so WHAT? I have no problem cybering with an 80-year-old man,*

*as long as he is smart, funny, and passionate . . . oh,
and can get me off.*

*I'm a 43-year-old handicapped man. What does it
[cybersex] hurt—it's my only way to have the experience of sex.*

Last, in this age of AIDS and STDs, cybersex offers a
viable alternative. It provides an option for people who
want to wait until marriage to have sex, and for those of us
who are celibate for any reason.

*Cyber is just something where you can forget about
knowing the person, making sure they don't have
HIV or AIDS (this *is* the '90s, isn't it?) or any other
disease. You can meet someone, type sweet nothings
onto their screen, and, well . . . go at it!*

The anonymity helps us get to a place of trust with a
cyberpartner that may be difficult in our real lives. We are
forced to learn how to communicate effectively with another person, to be brutally honest, to take things slowly
because of the medium. If you're single, these are all skills
that you can practice in a cyberrelationship, then use as
you form new relationships in your real life. If you're partnered, the same holds true. You learn to find your boundaries and stick to them, communicate better, and honor the
truth. Once you learn these skills on-line, testing them out
in your real-life relationship can only bring a couple closer
together.

CONTROL. All sexual relationships are based on power and control. Who's going to initiate? Who's going to be on top? Who's going to climax first? You get the idea. Most of the time, this is unspoken communication.

In cybersex, you have complete control over yourself, your movements, how far you're willing to go, even if you're going to stay on-line! From heading into a chat room to se- lect a partner to telling him or her what to do to you, you are in charge. Some say there's negotiation and partnership, but the truth is, for many, cybersex is simply about mastur- bation. And in order to climax to satisfaction, you have to be in control of what feels right to you. You select the per- son, the pace, the words, the details. You are desired, ca- ressed, and aroused by another. You get your needs met, and you fulfill your cyberpartner's.

Many, many folks try out D/s (dominance and submis- sion) techniques on-line. It's a great fantasy world where you find out if you like to be in control or be controlled, with a minimum of risk. Those who practice D/s in real life say the on-line power games are nothing like living in a 24/7 erotic power relationship, but hey, who would want to en- ter into a real-life one without trying it on for size? The Internet is the place to do it.

Again, you have to be careful, especially if you're look- ing to find out about submission, because many who hang around in these chat rooms really don't understand power erotics or the mutuality involved in creating a scene. But if you visit some of the sites I mention in Chapter Six: "Overcoming Sexual Inhibitions," you will find a more so- phisticated and considerate group. You can find specific information about how to enter a chat room as a dominant or a submissive at http://www.frugaldomme.com/dometiqu. htm. This is the Etiquette area of the **Frugal Domme** site.

HOW TO DO IT

There are two basic ways of approaching cybersex. The first is anonymous and casual. It's like going into a bar, picking up the first person you see, and going home with him. Age, appearance, personality—none of it matters. You just want to have wild, spontaneous sex and enjoy yourself. This is the easiest form of cybersex to find and engage in, no strings attached. You never know who your partner is, and you never have the same partner twice.

The quickest way to pick up a partner is in the **Internet Relay Chat (IRC)**, where you can find channels with names like Cybersex, Wild Sex, Sex on the Beach, Lovers Paradise, etc. To learn how to use IRC, head to the FAQs (frequently asked questions) at http://www.innotts.co.uk/~backup/ irc.html. You can find out the particulars of how to use the service, links to download software, and the basic commands to use once you're in a channel. When you first sign on to IRC, you are given a choice of channels (equivalent to chat rooms on other services), but you can also type in the "/list" command to get the full list of channels operating at any given moment.

There are also wild chat rooms on the paying services like **America Online** and **Compuserve**. On America Online, click on the People Connection, go to the Member

Rooms, and see if there's a room with an interesting name. There are also popular private rooms, but the names aren't listed. Someone has to tell you about one, or you can guess your best and try out names like Cybersex, Love, Kiss, KinkySex, etc. Compuserve also has a long-standing Human Sexuality Forum that is more informational and expert-driven than the open forums on IRC and AOL. The rooms in this forum, while sexually explicit, tend to be more sophisticated and mature.

You have to select a screen name or nickname to use. It's the name that others will know you by, so be mindful in selection. If you're looking for a quick pickup or a sexual exploration, say it in your name. Be creative—PickMeUp, Deliteful, HotMama, CuteButt, LoverBoy—are just a few of the names that jump to mind. Use your name to entice people to find out more about you.

On most services, you can also create a personal profile or join the member directory, where you can provide more specific information. Stay away from your real name and city, and head toward luscious, sensuous words that will show up in a quick search by other folks looking for a good time.

The classic scene is that anyone with a feminine-sounding name gets hit on within a second or two of signing on. Unfortunately, most of the opening lines are not very creative. You will hear a lot of the following:

- Do you want to cyber?
- Want to have sex with a 23/m?

- Mine's 10^1/$_2$ inches.
- Whisper if you want to cyber.
- Hey, honey, looking for a good time?
- How large are your boobs?

As you might guess, all of these lines are from men to women. Women don't seem to approach men in the same crass way . . . unless of course they are men pretending to be women. (Note: Keep your eyes open for this phenomenon. It's usually pretty easy to spot, as all the men do is change their names, not their tactics.)

Women tend to approach men with a more clever line, or by making small talk before jumping into the prospect of cybersex. And truth be told, men could learn a bit from this slower and more gracious manner. If a guy does approach with an ounce more tact than asking, "Wanna cyber?", he's got a decent chance of getting what he desires. After all, the women *are* in the cyberspace chat room, too, right?

Public rooms (and on AOL, some popular private rooms) are most commonly used to find potential partners. Then two (or more) people head off into private chat. The modes and mechanisms of private chat depend on which service you're on—so don't be afraid to use your "Help" command to learn the basics of your homebase. None of them are very difficult, but it helps to know a bit about the ins and outs of negotiating private chat so you don't give up all your control to your new partner.

In the Help area of any on-line service, you should be able to find information about how to ignore someone

133

who's bothering you in a public room or channel, as well as how to let the management know of a person who's causing perpetual problems. America Online, for instance, has simple "ignore features" that you can select to ignore instant messages, e-mail, or on-line chat from a particular person. Remember, someone who's bothering you is just looking for attention—rather than trying to rationalize, be civil, or threaten him, it's best to ignore him. That way, the attention is cut off, he's bored, he goes away, and you're left to enjoy your time on-line.

Many people like to exchange pics or gifs or photos before they get started. The visual stimulation can enhance the experience; sometimes it's an experience in and of itself. You should think about it seriously before you start exchanging pictures of yourself on the Internet. Once you send your picture "out there," it is no longer your property and can be passed from computer to computer like a virus. Not to scare you away from sharing photos, just making sure you don't enter the process naïvely.

If you're interested in sharing photos of yourself, you can purchase (or borrow) a digital camera, take the shots, then download them right onto your computer. They are then ready, willing, and able for digital exchange with another Internet user. If you're not feeling technologically savvy, you can use a regular snapshot, then scan it into your computer. You do need a piece of equipment called a scanner to do this, so if you don't have one, find a close friend who can keep your secret to help you. There are also services on-line that will scan photos for you, but I imagine privacy is not guaranteed. You could also go to a professional computer station in your neighborhood and use the equipment there to scan your photo yourself. Then you simply save it to a disk or mail it to yourself via e-mail.

It's up to you how much you're willing to expose in a photograph. You might want to take a series of photos depicting different moods and varying amounts of explicitness. That way you're in control, and can decide what type of photo to send depending on the person you're cybering with and your comfort level at the moment. Again, it is not wise to send a completely nude photo of yourself, face included, to someone you just met on-line. While the experience can be fun and titillating, you have to be smart about what you're doing, just like you are in the rest of your life.

Some people like to exchange a few words and then get down to business. Others like to get to know you a little bit before taking off their clothes. It all depends. The trick is to set the boundaries before you start. Are you hoping to start a relationship based on the sharing of erotica? Are you looking to have casual, anonymous sex? Make sure you're both on the same page. While it seems cybersex doesn't involve feelings, there *is* another human being on the other end of the screen.

One man says this about getting to know his cyber-partners:

I love to cyber; I think it's great. The only thing is I can't cyber with someone I have never talked to before. Someone sent me a message and went right into cybering without asking my name or if I even wanted to. I know it's probably silly since the person you cyber

*with is a stranger, but I would just like to have a regu-
lar conversation first. I guess some reality does play a
part here, because I would not have sex (in real life)
with someone whose name I didn't even know.*

It all depends on what you're looking for. If you do exchange information, don't be naïve. It's important not to
give out identifying information like your full name (which
on some services is attached to your account, so beware),
details about where you live or work or about any family
members. And remember, you *can* say anything you want,
so if you've always wanted to be a busty blonde or a hunky
weightlifter, now's your chance. Some people like you
to describe yourself (especially if you're not sharing photos), so this is your opportunity to get creative and have
some fun.

The second type of cybersex, typing interactive stories
with the intent of arousal, can be found on bulletin boards
and in forums across the Net. One of the easiest places to
start is the **alt.sex BBS** (bulletin board service). You can
find an entire listing of your choices within alt.sex at
http://www.sunsite.unc.edu/usenet-i/hier-s/alt.sex.html.
You will find everything from leather to large women and
the people who love them. The gem is the alt.sex.stories
BBS, which includes subtopics like gay, hetero, and moderated stories. The unfortunate fact is that many of these BBS
services have degenerated lately into large advertisements
for pornographic sites; but if you're patient, you can still
find some great stories in the mix. Another common BBS to
find interactive erotica is **rec.arts.erotica**. You can find the

FAQs and all relevant information about the newsgroup at http://www.non.com/news.answers/erotica-faq.html.

Other places to find public interactive stories include just about any forum that has a fantasy area, or a sex and relationships section. Once someone gets started writing, it's hard to stop them! A good place to find current sites of interactive erotica is on **Yahoo**. If you go to http://www.yahoo.com, then follow this train of clicks, you'll be all set—Arts: Humanities: Literature: Genres: Web Published Fiction: Adult Fiction. There's quite an extensive list of amateur fiction there with descriptions of which ones invite user contributions.

Another large community of forums and chat that supports "forum cybersex" is **Bianca's Smut Shack**. You can find a variety of folks writing on-line erotic stories for each other at http://www.members.bianca.com/mforums/erotica/. The range is diverse, from smutty to excellent. If you search awhile, they do have a large, sophisticated community, so you're most likely to find what you're seeking.

CONCLUSION

There are a myriad of reasons why people engage in cybersex. Fantasy and desire rule the pack. In the world of cybersex, you can live out your fantasies and fulfill your sexual desires behind the safety of your computer screen. You can have casual sex or a romantic encounter. You can build trust and intimacy with another person and explore the deepest parts of your sexuality, or you can have many brief affairs with folks of different ages, genders, ethnicities, sizes, physical abilities, etc. You can have consensual safe sex without fear of pregnancy or disease. You can explore your sexual boundaries and push beyond them. You can explore the nooks and crannies of your body and awaken your sexuality. And when you're finished, you can turn off your computer and use the skills you've acquired in your real life.

Engaging in cybersex in a responsible way can broaden your sexual horizons, and if you carry that forward into your face-to-face relationships, it can enrich your sexual experience. Whether in a long-term relationship and looking for some new stimulation or single and practicing for when you meet your special someone, cybersex can do it for you. You have choices about whether you want to chat or to participate in telling interactive erotic stories; but no matter which you choose, you'll find a large community of folks already engaged and welcoming of a newcomer. Just remember the cautionary word of advice—the world of cybersex is all fantasy. If you can bridge the gap between the virtual and the real, it's an incredible tool; if you can't, it can become an unhealthy addiction.

If you read on to the next chapter, "Hot Monogamy," you'll find ideas for making sex with a long-term partner wild and exciting again. It's not too difficult if you use the Internet as a tool, and if you and your partner are both open to the endless possibilities. While this chapter focused on exploring your fantasies and desires on the computer alone, the next will give you ideas about how to do it *with* a partner and make all your sexual dreams come true!

ANNOTATED SITE LISTING

http://www.frugaldomme.com/dometiqu.htm This is the Etiquette area of the Frugal Domme site.

http://www.innotts.co.uk/~backup/irc.html FAQs (frequently asked questions) about Internet Relay Chat (IRC).

http://www.sunsite.unc.edu/usenet-i/ hier-s/alt.sex.html Listing of the topics in the alt.sex Bulletin Board Service (BBS).

http://www.non.com/news.answers/ erotica-faq.html FAQs and all relevant information about the alt.rec.erotica newsgroup.

http://www.yahoo.com Follow this train of clicks— Arts: Humanities: Literature: Genres: Web Published Fiction: Adult Fiction for erotica listings on the Internet.

http://www.members.bianca.com/mforums/ erotica/ Erotica on the Bianca's Smut Shack site.

HOT MONOGAMY

Hot monogamy. For many of us, it's a contradiction in terms. After years with the same person, sex can definitely get boring. But there are a certain number of couples who are always wearing a consummate grin when they're together. If you ask them, you'll hear there's no magic pill or potion; just hard work, energy, and prioritizing sex in the relationship. Any respectable marriage counselor, on-line or off, will tell you the same thing.

First, it's important that you honestly assess your relationship, and decide for yourself whether it's simply the sex that needs improving or whether you need to do some other work on your relationship before you start adding the Virtual Twisted Butterfly to your sexual repertoire.

Once you take a long hard look at your relationship, if you realize it's simply a matter of lack of imagination and creativity, then the rest of the chapter is for you. The computer can be an invaluable tool, if you know how to use it effectively. The anonymity of the medium allows couples to express themselves in ways that they might be too afraid or embarrassed to confront face-to-face. It allows room for exploration of things that might have been whispered about, but not discussed in any tangible sort of way.

For instance, in this chapter, I'll tell you all about:

- Sending sexy e-mails to and receiving them from your partner
- The best sites for checking out erotica on-line together
- Using chat rooms to exhibit your sexual prowess with your partner and role-play your fantasies
- Learning sexual enhancement techniques from an on-line course
- Visiting erotic Web sites with your partner
- Renewing your commitment vows to each other virtually

But before we move into the virtual world, it's time for you to take a look at your relationship and determine whether there's a problem that needs to be solved, or if the problems are simply a matter of familiarity over time.

KNOW YOURSELF . . . AND YOUR RELATIONSHIP!

Give yourself a few minutes to answer the following questions, and take note of anything that strikes a chord:

- Do you enjoy sex with your partner?
- If not, have you *ever* enjoyed sex with your partner?
- Do you tell your partner when you feel satisfied sexually?
- Are you having less, more, or the same amount of sex in your relationship than when you first met?
- If less, when did the sex in your relationship start to get routine and boring?
- Did something change over the last few months or years, or do you feel you've always had a passionless sex life?
- Has something changed in your, or your partner's, life recently? (A new job, loss of a job, stress, illness, family problems, etc.)
- Has something changed in both of your lives in the past few months or years? (A move, a new baby, a death, problems with a teenager, etc.)
- Has one of you gained or lost a lot of weight?
- Is one of you fast approaching midlife, and worried to death about it?
- How well do you and your partner communicate?
- Do you feel your partner has a clue you're dissatisfied sexually?

After you've answered these questions, think about how you and your partner interact. If there's been a major life event in your relationship over the last year or so, you can expect your sex life is going to change. If you find you're angry at your partner over something other than sex, it's likely that you're using sex as the bargaining chip to resolve other problems. In either case, a few sessions with a family counselor may be in order before you turn to the computer as a panacea.

If you're still not sure where you stand, you can head out to the Web to secure insight into how you measure up sexually compared to other couples. These quizzes are similar to those you'd find in a national women's magazine, except after you answer the questions, you get instantaneous results. Here's an example of a quiz I wrote for **Thrive** in the name of my alter ego, Delilah. For the full quiz, go to the site at http://www.thriveonline.com/sex/delilah/index.html. This should help you determine how you fare in the ever elusive world of sex with a longtime partner.

How many times a month do you have sex?
1) not every month, if at all
2) a few times a month
3) two to three times a week
4) more than four times a week

About 36 percent of American men and women have sex a few times a month. While "a few" may sound vague, a few times a month is definitely more than twice a year.

How long did your last sexual event last (in minutes, that is!)?
   1) 15 minutes or less
   2) 15 minutes to one hour
   3) one hour or more
   4) didn't have one

About 70 percent of Americans make love for 15 minutes to one hour. Across all boundaries—gender, age, marital status, education, religion, race, and ethnicity—this is the time frame most heterosexuals work within.

Have you seen an X-rated movie or bought a sex magazine, gone to a topless bar, or engaged in cybersex in the last twelve months?
   1) watched an X-rated movie or bought sexually explicit reading materials
   2) visited a topless or nude bar
   3) had cybersex
   4) some combination of the above
   5) never even considered the possibility

Of the more conventional "autoerotic" materials (movies, topless joints, books and magazines, sex toys, 900 numbers), 41 percent of men and 16 percent of women have used one or another in the last year at least once. People who explore erotica, whether on-line, on the phone, or in a topless bar, are people who find sex sexy—they're the most sexually active, and find a variety of sexual experiences appealing.

How do you fare? If you're like most folks out there, you're middle-of-the-road. At this point, if you've determined there's nothing catastrophic going on in your relationship, the cause of your sexual boredom or dissatisfaction is not transition-related, and you're just not having exciting sex anymore, you deserve a hearty congratulations! Your problems are the very same ones many other couples have after years of being together. Read on.

What I'm about to describe is a way of adding spice to your partnership that is incredibly '90s. When you've been together for a long time, and begin to take your relationship for granted, sex can become routine. What the Internet can do for you is bring back the element of mystery. Enter the anonymity of the computer—and *voilà*, you have simply added another dimension to your relationship.

Remember when you first met? All right, I know it's difficult, but try! Part of the intrigue was discovering who and what the other person was about. Over time, the playfulness, discovery, and mystery subside into daily chores and the drudgery of cooking dinner and changing diapers. The Internet, as a sexual tool, can help add back that element of surprise and intrigue into your relationship. Let's get started!

SEXY E-MAILS

Technologically speaking, one of the easiest ways a couple can spice up their sex life is by sending sexy e-mails to each other. It's not that much different from one of the most traditional ways of courting—writing love notes. In the 1500s, King Henry VIII wrote long, flowing love letters to Anne Boleyn; in the 1700s, Voltaire penned a spicy note to Olympe Dunoyer; and in the 1900s, Franz Kafka wrote thousands of beautiful letters to his beloved, Felice Bauer.

Love letters are thousands of times better than phone calls because you can't reread a phone call, savoring it by day and memorizing it by night. Second, it means more to your partner that you've taken the time to spill your heart out in words. And third, if you write a sexy e-mail to your partner, you're likely to get a letter in return, and then you too can have the thrill of finding not another piece of junk mail in your box, but a red-hot letter. It's worked for centuries!

To write a sexy e-mail to your lover, all you need is access to any on-line service provider that will give you an e-mail account. (There are several that even offer free e-mail, with limited access to other on-line services.)

Haven't you always wished you could talk dirty to your partner? Maybe you don't do it because you're afraid you won't be able to look at yourself in the mirror the next morning. In the anonymity of cyberspace—the land where everything is done virtually—you don't have to worry about how you look when you do it or how you feel afterward.

"But what will I say?" you ask hesitantly. Anything you've always wanted to say to your partner, but were afraid, unwilling, or too embarrassed to say out loud. Start by writing a note to let your honey know you love him, and that there's a special treat waiting at home, as soon as he shuts off the computer. (This is where the lingerie, roses, candlelight dinners—all those real-life things that conjure images of sex and romance—come into play.)

Your e-mail sets the stage for anticipation and mystery. Especially if the e-mail is unexpected—try sending it to her business account during the day. You're sure to make a splash in the middle of a string of e-mails about meetings, stock reports, and staff problems!

The truth is, setting the stage for lovemaking is incredibly important. A sexy e-mail can do just that—set the stage for an extraordinary lovemaking session. In between the sexy e-mail you send and your night of passion-filled extravagance, think positive thoughts in anticipation. Avoid thinking about your partner's faults; instead focus on all the reasons you've chosen to be with him. If you find yourself fantasizing, turn your thoughts to fantasies of the best sex you've ever had together.

Here's an example of a simple sexy e-mail a man sent to his wife to pique her sexual interest. Note that this didn't take a long time to compose, nor did this man take a huge risk in sending it to his wife. Remember, most people are turned on by compliments, especially if they're sincere.

Honey,
It's so sexy to see the expressions on your face when we're making love. It turns me on so much I almost can't control myself. I'd love to see you in ecstasy later tonight. What do you say?
Love, Mark

TAKING E-MAILS ONE STEP FURTHER

You've sent a number of short, enticing notes to your partner, and now you need something new to do with your
e-mail account. Here's your chance to go wild, become an
amateur writer of erotica—let your partner know what
you'd *really* like to do to her sexually. You can also send
a pre-made erotic card, or if you're just feeling mushy, a
cyber–greeting card.

If your partner is a hopeless romantic, start by writing a poem, or quoting one of her favorite poets. Kahlil
Gibran and e.e. cummings come to mind immediately,
both of whose poetry you can find on-line at public sites,
**Of love, marriage, children, and giving: Selections from
The Prophet by Kahlil Gibran** (http://www.gn.apc.org/
inquirer/gibran.html) and at **UC Berkeley's gopher service**
(gopher://gopher.ocf.berkeley.edu:70/11/Library/Poetry/
EECummings).

If you're feeling uninspired or shy, you can find many
places on-line where you can send romantic greeting cards
via e-mail. Two on-line card shops are **Awesome Cybercard** (http://www.marlo.com/card.htm) and **ByteSize
Greetings** (http://www.bytesizegreetings.com/). If you
want to up the ante a bit, there are always the erotic cards at
Sexy Cards Online (http://www.sexycards.com/), which
mainly has cards of naked women.

If you're feeling your creative juices flowing, try exploring your new "career" as an amateur author of erotica. I
think the personalized versions of sexy e-mails are the most
effective. Send all the electronic greeting cards you like, but

a message with everything you've always fantasized about from your real-life partner can send your love life to the moon! How to get started? Do a little Web surfing, and find some of the sites authored by other amateur writers of erotica. Read what others have written. Or better yet, visit **Victoria's Web site.** Victoria is a mother of two, teacher, and amateur writer of erotica. Not only does she share some of her own writing on her site, but she lists both real and virtual resources for beginners (http://www.accelnet.com/victoria/).

Here's an example from a couple who use sexy e-mails as a regular part of their sex life. This is the middle of a series of e-mails a woman sent to her husband during the day, and believe you me, they had great sex that night after work!

Dear Jake,
Last night when we were sleeping together, I had this dream. I can't get it out of my mind, and I want to share it with you before the day's over.

A vision on the side of the road catches my eye. A hitchhiker. The hitchhiker is you—your height, your weight, your coloring. He's standing with most of his weight on his left leg, his right thumb stuck out in the breeze. He is wearing a tank top and tight jeans; his smooth chest and the muscles in his arms gleam with sweat from the summer sun. He carries a knapsack, and most of his face is obscured behind mirrored sunglasses.

I pass him, then edge the convertible over to the shoulder of the road. I look in the mirror and see him running toward me. He stops as he gets to the passenger side and looks down at me, not knowing whether or not to get in. I smile and he knows. Without a word, he gets in and I pull the car back onto the road.

We ride in silence. I can see he is looking me over. I turn my head to him, and his eyes come up from my legs to meet my eyes. He smiles. It's a slightly crooked smile.

Only half of the blinking motel light is working, so only "MOT" is lit up. I pull up to the office and within minutes I'm back with a key. I drive to the back side of the motel where the room is and get out. He follows silently.

The room is plain: dirty beige walls, worn brown carpet, shabby torn curtains. I don't care about any of those things. All I want it to have is a bed and an air conditioner. I switch on the air and lock the dead bolt. When I turn from the door, he is standing behind me, only inches away, smiling. He takes off his sunglasses and lightly touches my face with his hand. Suddenly, he pushes me against the door, kissing me fervently, holding my arms behind my back. I'm defenseless, but I know he won't hurt me; you never do. You only want the same thing I do.

He takes my hand and leads me over to the bed. I undress myself, then lie back on the mattress. I watch as he pulls his top over his head, and unzips his jeans. He wears nothing under them. I am pleased with what I see. "Touch yourself," he says quietly.

My fingers probe into the warm, pink flesh, and I gasp softly at the feeling. He opens his knapsack and pulls out a bottle of tequila. He takes a big swig and watches me for a few minutes, rubbing himself at the same time. He walks around the bed, taking occasional drinks from the bottle, viewing me from different angles. By the time he has gone completely around the bed, and is back up at the headboard, I am tired of playing with myself. I reach out and touch him. "This is what I want."

Honey, what time will you be home tonight? I'm so hot just thinking about this dream.
Love, Deirdre

The thing about sexy e-mails is once you get started and find the right rhythm, things can get quite steamy. Each of you can up the ante a bit by writing the next e-mail, describing what you'd like to do to each other, or taking a fictional stance by telling an erotic story to each other, over time, via e-mail. The privacy is evident—no one else ever has to read your tales of lust and love except the person for whose eyes it's meant. (If this idea intrigues you, then you might want to keep a personal e-mail account separate from your work account, for obvious reasons.)

ALL KINDS OF EROTICA

A simple way to spice up your sex life is to surf the Web for erotic images together. While in truth, most sites offering erotica are more bark than bite, it could be an interesting evening or two searching for sites to give you ideas for new things you can do as a couple. Of course, they could also give you a good laugh (due to many of the sites' inauthenticity), but hey, a good laugh can spur you right into the bedroom!

Most of the sites give you something enticing to get you to click further into them, of course, seeing more advertisers along the way while you wait and wait for the photographs to arrive on your screen. People I've spoken to have said the same thing—by the time they get to a photo, the excitement's pretty much over. That is, unless you're waiting with your partner. Why not spend some time caressing each other and doing to each other whatever it is you're waiting to see? Then you can compare and contrast when the pictures actually do download!

There are a few decent sites with soft-porn images and erotica out there on the Internet, with more popping up every day. A good place to start your search is at the **Persian Kitty** site (http://www.persiankitty.com). This site, updated daily, has links to many of the finer sex sites in cyberspace. They're categorized as free sites with images, free sites with amateur pictures, pics of men, pics of women, erotic stories, interesting sites, phone/video sex, and more. Because it's so comprehensive, you and your partner know exactly what you're going to get with each click.

Another fascinating site is **Retro Raunch** (http://www.retroraunch.com). It contains "a century of smut," including more than 5,000 erotic photos of women and men through the ages. There is a monthly service fee to get all the materials, including the rambunctious '20s and '30s, the pristine '50s, and even some great '70s nostalgia. The key to this site is that the photos are all from the era before porn was glamorous and lucrative, so these poses feel more genuine and sexy.

Another great place to visit with your partner is the **Libido** site (http://www.sensualsource.com/libido). It considers itself the Journal of Sex and Sensibility, and comes across most definitely as a highbrow pornographic site. It includes fiction, poetry, and, of course, photos of people engaging in sexual activity.

The beauty of these sites is that they are all intentionally women-friendly, so you and your partner can take some time to explore them without feeling offended by the content—you can have a healthy, sexy experience and still be a feminist. In fact, many of the sites are managed by women who, like you and me, are just searching for some new ways to spice it up!

One married woman's comments on looking at erotica on the Net:

Give me an X-rated film or an erotic Web site any day and my husband and I will have a great night of sex.

*It is a big turn-on for me. I just discovered how much
fun erotica on the Web can be. In addition to getting
turned on by looking, sometimes you can pick up new
ideas too. Try it—you might like it!*

And if you want to have that real-life feeling of desire
restored, think about sending an erotic pic to your partner
via e-mail. All you have to do is take a photo of yourself (or
have a good friend do it for you) in lingerie, or flexing your
muscles, scan it into a computer, save it, then attach the file
in an e-mail to your honey. Talk about bringing back the
excitement—especially if you're usually a reserved person,
the surprise alone should be enough to get the fires started.
You can also start leaving "compromising" photos of yourself around the house (if you don't have kids), or in your
partner's briefcase or underwear drawer, and mailing photos to him or her in plain white envelopes. Sending photos
on the Net can start you well on your way to a greatly improved sex life with your partner.

USING VIRTUAL PLACES

Most of us know chat rooms as crazy, chaotic, hard-to-
figure-out places where people on-line seem to congregate.
If you've ever been in one, you know that there seems to
be erratic, disjointed conversation, and lots of idle pickup
lines.

If you're creative, there are ways to use a chat room to
spice up your sex life in a monogamous relationship. Let's

take a sexuality/relationship-oriented chat room to start. You go in, people are idly chatting about anything from laundry to sports, to how they're going to score tonight. If you and your partner drop in and feel like being exhibitionists in a safe, nonthreatening way, now is your chance.

Start talking to each other, as if you were alone. Begin your verbal seduction. Pay close attention to each other, while watching everyone else's reactions at the same time. And if you're good, everyone will react! Undress each other with your words, and have some fun. It's great if you have two computers and two accounts, but if you don't, you can always choose a chat name that insinuates two people—for instance, "CuplaLuvBirds" or "2OfUs" or "Married& Sexy."

If you're feeling more private, most Web sites that have chat communities also give you the ability to create a private room on-line. They are usually used by people who have picked each other up virtually to enjoy a sexual liaison. But there's no reason why you and your honey can't use it to your own ends—that is, marital sexual bliss.

What you need to do is look around on the chat room page for a button or some text that says something to the effect of "Create a private room." Then click on it. It will ask you to name your room, so be as creative as you like, because as long as you don't click where it says, "Allow the public in," this room is just for your personal invited guest.

Being sexual in a private chat room works well when one or both of you are on the road; during lunchtime at the office (if no one looks over your shoulder); or late at night, after the kids have gone to bed, from two separate rooms in the house. The basic analogy is the "quickie," and we all know how much they can spice up a boring sex life. Without much effort, and without the intense intimacy necessary for making love, having sex in a chat room takes a short time and is perfect for when you and your partner want to connect briefly and lovingly.

Once in the room, there will be instructions on how to invite your honey to join you. You do need two separate computers to pull this off gracefully, because while it may work to take turns typing, it would certainly be quite cumbersome. And using one Internet account definitely won't work if you're in different rooms of the house, or different parts of the country.

Having sex via the computer in a private room allows you to re-create desire in your relationship, desire that may be waning or even absent when you look at each other in real life. The abstractness, the objectivity, of the computer screen allows you to bring the passion back into your relationship in a whole new way.

Also, because many of us are shy or hung-up about sex, the anonymity of the computer offers a safe place to be sexual without any of the accompanying guilt. The influence our family and society in general have had on our sexual mores, the patterns we've established with our partners, the natural embarrassment we humans have when we try to talk about sex in any sort of real way all tend to disappear with the flicker of a computer screen. Something about the computer helps to break down the barriers, and allows you and your longtime partner to experiment and fully realize your sexuality.

Once you get into an on-line chat room, you have the opportunity to experiment with your partner in a safe, trusting manner. Many couples try role-playing for the first time. You can create your own roles, or use one of the more common themes that arise among heterosexual couples:

- Virgin and seducer
- Prostitute and john
- Dominatrix and submissive
- Servant and demanding employer
- Strict schoolteacher and naughty student
- Hospital patient and horny nurse or doctor
- Older man, younger woman
- Older woman, younger man
- Captain Jean-Luc Picard and Counselor Troy

The possibilities for role-playing on-line are endless, and just as in sexy e-mails, the more personalized they are, the more likely you and your partner are going to get the stimulation you're looking for from the experience.

> *I love seduction. It's my favorite game, and I like to play it on-line in a chat room with my lover. I type in very explicit language, using earthy words, describing the slow buildup of erotic tension we're each feeling. I like to make promises to her that I plan to keep later on when we're together in the flesh. I explain in delicious detail all the things that I want to do to her. Then, later, when we're alone, and I'm fulfilling my promises, I love to talk as nasty as possible. And if she*

agrees, I whisper in her ear, urging her on, moaning and purring my passion. The setup in the chat room really makes for intense arousal in our real lives. There's nothing else like it.

If you're having a hard time understanding the premise, take a step back and picture this. After the kids are asleep, you and your partner both go on-line and agree to meet at your favorite site. But you go on-line under another name, without telling him. You show up and start making sexual advances toward him in public. He's clearly turned on by the experience, and has an idea, although he is not sure, that it's you. You continue to tease, as he types that he's waiting for his wife to join him. You consider asking his wife to join you, too . . . causing him undue stress and increasing his excitement level. Then you invite him into a private room, suggesting that you can both keep a lookout for his wife. Once in the room, you continue to tease, flirt, seduce him, dropping hints along the way so he realizes it's you and he can really let loose and enjoy. Doesn't sound half bad, does it? Once you're both completely turned on, you can rendezvous in the bedroom and have great sex.

This is such a perfect scenario. You've been together for years and have gotten used to each other in every aspect of your life. You know every part of your spouse's body in great detail, and sex has become routine. Then you go into a chat room and bring in the unknown, a feeling that hasn't been kindled since you first met. As they said in the old Alka-Seltzer commercial, "Try it, you'll like it."

Another option would be to create an ambience in a

private room—one that isn't possible in your busy daily life. For instance, maybe a few years ago you and your partner went on a great vacation together in Hawaii. It was the most relaxed you'd been in years together, and the sex was great. It's been difficult, if not impossible, for you two to recreate the stupendous time you had together.

Enter the private chat room. You can name the room appropriately. Something like Caribbean Paradise, or Hawaii Dreams, or London Lust. Then invite your significant other into the room and imagine. Make sure you're both as relaxed as you can be while sitting at the computer. Put on some soothing music, headphones even, ideally music you heard while on vacation. Then start by typing, "Remember when we got to Honolulu, that first breath of fresh, tropic air wafting in, the breeze sailing through our hair?" Your wife can respond, "Yes, I do. And then we went on to savor our first tropical fruit drink—mango, rice milk, sugar, and cinnamon—it was so delicious." By now, you've got three of your senses involved: the sound of music, the feel of the wind, and the taste of tropical fruit. That's a good start . . . it's up to you and your honey to take it from here.

A private chat room is also a good place for you and your partner to "live out" some of your fantasies. In addition to role-playing, you can set the mood to establish a sexual tryst in a place you've always imagined. This can include places like a beach on a deserted island, or the hood of a car in a thunderstorm. It can involve other players—the doorman of your building, the taxi driver who took you to dinner last night, the security guard at Kmart, the female police officer in your town, whatever. It's easier and brings up less real-life tension if you choose someone either completely fictional or someone you're both familiar with, but not on any sort of intimate terms. You don't want to destroy the moment by bringing in the idea that you've fantasized about, say, your wife's sister for the last few years. (I know it's obvious, but still worth stating.)

Many couples who have considered a threesome to be the ultimate sexual turn-on have been able to use the chat rooms to explore this fantasy more fully. Without going into details (see Chapter Seven: "Beyond the Picket Fence"), couples who like the idea of a *ménage à trois*, but are uncomfortable living it out in real life, can use a private chat room to play with this fantasy without the jealousy and insecurity that come along with living it out in real time. Many men (and yes, it is men who are more likely to have this fantasy) are turned on enough by the idea of talking to their wife on-line about the possibility—who would you choose to be the third, what would you do with him or her if we were all together, etc.—so the idea of having to do it in real life becomes secondary. In other words, for most people, it is just as much fun to realize the fantasy virtually as it is to realize the prospect of doing it in real life.

One last idea (for now!) for what you can do alone together in a chat room on-line: a verbal striptease. You describe to your partner what clothing you're taking off at any given moment while typing to her in the room. And if you take the clothes off as you type (tricky, but certainly possible), then you can even heighten the experience. One partner does all the typing, while the other reads, watches, absorbs. After your clothes are off, describe where you are touching yourself, how you are touching yourself, and how it's feeling to you. Truth be told, you don't even have to be doing anything—your partner sitting in another room (or across the world) can be reading and imagining what your beautiful body looks like and enjoying herself.

What if your partner is not very experimental? It's important to remember that the two of you are simply exploring your sexual options in a safe way together on-line, privately. If your partner has expressed prior reluctance to try something new, try discussing the cyberoptions with him before you start out. As the medium is familiar (if you're both comfortable using computers in other parts of your life), on-line sexual experimentation might not be so intimidating, especially because you can enjoy it together, with the computer screen as a sort of neutral dividing line.

The best analogy I can think of is masturbation. Most men and many women masturbate alone, but if one partner suggests masturbating together, the ante is upped significantly. Masturbation is something you do alone, you don't know what you look like, you're not sure you want to share it, and you're too embarrassed about your own sexuality and pleasure to show your satisfaction to another person.

Enter the computer—which naturally lends itself to opening up the imagination and creative spirit. Because you don't have to see each other one-on-one, you can let loose and experiment unabashedly. The most important thing is that you keep real-life communication open along the way. Always remember to express when you're turned on as well as when you're uncomfortable. Since most of us aren't mind readers, feedback during sex helps build trust and intimacy, and will lead you and your partner toward a better, more satisfying sex life.

THE POWER OF TOUCH

I don't know anyone who doesn't like a good massage. But it seems like unless we pay a professional, we're always asking, sometimes pleading with, our partners to massage us. I would venture a guess that if you and your partner were schooled in the power of erotic massage, it would become a more natural part of your sexual repertoire. Erotic massage begins as a full body rub, and then focuses in on the genitals, extending and multiplying orgasms in response.

For the best instructions I've seen about how to give an erotic massage, see the site **How to Give an Erotic Massage** (http://www.sexuality.org/erotmass.html). It's laid out into three parts: how to give and receive, how to help your partner relax, and how to help your partner achieve extended or multiple orgasms as part of their massage. From guidelines on creating the setting, to which massage oils to use, to keeping the lines of communication open, the instructions are all-inclusive. Here's an excerpt describing the transition of the massage from general body rub to genital stimulation:

> *After relaxing your partner's back, legs, and feet, have him or her turn over. Massage the chest, arms, and*

hands. Then glide down to the legs. It's OK to brush the genitals when going down to the legs. After finishing the fronts of the legs and feet, glide back up and slowly brush over the genitals, teasing them. This teasing process can be drawn out by brushing the inner thighs near the genitals, very lightly touching the pubic region, etc.

Look into your partner's eyes, while cradling his or her genitals, and ask your partner's permission to go further. "May I?" is a nice way of putting it (and by the way, it's perfectly OK for the receiving partner to respond, "In a few minutes . . ."). The rest of the massage will focus on the genitals, with periodic sweeps up and down the body to spread, balance, and integrate the sensations.

Partners can take turns being the giver and the receiver so no one has all work and no play. Try this once and it's likely to become a regular part of your sex play.

CYBERSEX UNIVERSITY

Sometimes you need a bit more than someone else's words telling you how to enhance your sex life. There are courses offered around the country by professional sex therapists and counselors in how to create an intimate, romantic, sexually satisfying love relationship. The courses have titles such as "Heart of Relating" and "PAIRS—Practical

Application of Intimate Relationships Skills." There are also videos available in which you can listen to a lecture, watch couples role-play the new techniques, and learn how to improve your own communication and relationship skills.

If you don't want to invest the money in a course or workshop (upward of $500 per person), or you're too embarrassed to show up in person, or there just isn't one offered in your area, there are a few courses you can explore on-line to gain the same knowledge. For example, you can try an on-line marriage-enhancement course, or a course in learning new ways to please your lover.

It's easy to find a number of courses designed to teach you the skills, attitudes, and approaches that make for relationship success. They are often taught by experienced couples' therapists or counselors. On many of these sites, you can also find a supportive community of like-minded people to help understand and improve your relationship. In the chat rooms and on the message boards, people share their experiences, their trials, and their tribulations honestly but anonymously.

One of the newer sites offering this type of service is called **Learn Well Resources** (http://www.learnwell.org/~edu/connect.shtml). When you arrive at the site, in the Marriage Resources area, you'll find Unit One, a series of questions about your marriage you can think about and answer on-line. Once you've completed the questionnaire, you submit it electronically. It's reviewed by two licensed therapists, and if you're accepted into the course, it's $39.00 for the next two units, consisting of surveys, exercises, and skills-building techniques to help you improve your marriage. Their goal is to help you strengthen your relationship step-by-step over time and to avoid and prevent unhealthy conflicts, divorce, and violence.

Another great site is the **Whole Family Center** (http://www.wholefamily.com/maritalcenter). The goals of their twelve-session marital-enhancement course are to:

- Restore passion and romance to your marriage
- Learn how to create marital friendship
- Discover skills to resolve marital conflicts creatively (including sexual conflicts)

Over the span of twelve weeks, for $35.00 a couple or $25.00 a person, you get written materials and practice exercises, a weekly chat with a psychotherapist, RealAudio mini-lectures (using an on-line broadcast system), and interactive discussion groups with other participants. Here's what one couple had to say about the course:

This on-line course just about saved our marriage. There were so many things my husband and I were afraid to discuss face-to-face (like not having enough sex). And we most certainly were not going to see a counselor locally—everyone knows us! Being able to explore our difficulties together, realize that other couples have the same problems, and get professional guidance on-line helped us to break through the blocks in our relationship. And now we have sex so regularly, it's as if we just met!

In addition to the twelve-week course, the Whole Family Center offers on-line marital counseling and sex therapy. The on-line counseling is short-term, goal-oriented therapy in which you fill out a personal questionnaire about your relationship, and pay $30.00 for a response from a licensed therapist.

The sex therapy area at the Whole Family Center offers a place to ask your questions of a licensed sex therapist and articles to read for enrichment, as well as a RealAudio piece where you and your partner have an opportunity to solve hypothetical problems other couples have. It's very interesting and informative to see if both you and your partner respond to the problems in the same way—an extraordinary learning tool.

For a more lighthearted version, take a look at the **Partnership Horoscopes** site (http://www.lucknet.com/personal/combo.html) where you can chart both your and your partner's astrological natal charts to give you insight into the past, present, and future of your relationship. And, on the racier side, there are CD-ROMs available for purchase on-line to provide the tools you need to spice up your sex life. There's **Dr. Ruth's CD-ROM Encyclopedia of Sex** (http://www.drruth.com). And, for some serious action, consider purchasing one of the hottest adult CD-ROM games, "Interactive Sex Therapy" from **Romdezvous.com** (http://www.romdezvous.com/www45.html). On the CD-ROM, a scene is described by a sex therapist, and then played out for you and your partner to watch. You then answer specific questions about the sexual role-play, which the doctor interprets to give you insight into your strengths and weaknesses as a relationship partner.

I imagine more and more sites with on-line sexuality and relationship courses will be cropping up over the next year or so, as therapists realize the potential of this medium for solving the complex, seemingly embarrassing sexual dilemmas confronting many married couples.

PLEDGE YOUR LOVE TO THE WORLD

If you are an incurable romantic, check this out: It's possible for you to renew your vows virtually, and create a Web page entirely devoted to your relationship. Believe it or not, there have even been virtual weddings and anniversary parties! (Much cheaper than real-life ones . . .)

Rather than tout the businesses that do well with the cybercrowd, I'd rather just throw out the concept. Imagine this: You've been married for x number of years. Things have ebbed and flowed, but through it all, it's clear you're going to stay together. And you want to tell the world. You can do this very simply—find out from your on-line service provider how much Web space comes with your account, then ask a techno-geek friend to help you put up your photos, vows, and memories. (Or you could always hire a personal Web consultant to help you, but you're moving into a pricier category now.) For an example, head to **A Celebration of Kamara Colvard's and Scott Hirni's Wedding Day** (http://www.localnet.com/~rkeinc/

amore.htm). On this couple's site, you'll find a poem honoring their commitment and the story of their betrothal. You can also sign their guest book with a greeting or download a movie for *your* loved one.

Another way to go is to buy an on-line create-a-vow kit (under $30.00), where you and your spouse choose from selected quotes, essays, and poems and put together a personalized piece for your renewal ceremony. You can find a free sample at **Elect Press** (http://www.electpress.com/loveandromance/page45.htm). The advantage to doing this on-line is that you can cut-and-paste the various phrases and quotes and test them out without much effort. You can then use your vows in your virtual ceremony, in your real-life celebration, or read them to each other in your own private ceremony.

If you want to go the more advanced route, you can pay a service to help you plan your anniversary or renewal ceremony through the Internet. Depending on the service, there are a variety of offerings, including:

- On-line invitations and RSVPs
- Information about hotel accommodations near the real-life ceremony site
- Directions to and from the affair
- On-line backgrounders about the couple
- On-line guest book for your friends and loved ones who visit the site
- On-line list of gift ideas and suggestions
- On-line photos of the ceremony, party, and second honeymoon (after the fact, of course!)

- Virtual slide shows to take you and yours down memory lane

It's pretty incredible what you can find on the Net. There are even a few folks who will officiate an on-line ceremony, so *all* of your friends and family can be there. So far, the on-line weddings have been few and far between (and well covered by the media, I might add).

But a renewal ceremony? That's something altogether revolutionary. And since it's less likely people will travel long distances for a second marriage ceremony, the Internet is a likely place to hold it—the majority of your computer-enabled friends and family can attend. All your guests need is a modem and an on-line service provider, or a friend who is hooked up. All you need is someone around who has Internet coding skills (html—hypertext mark-up language) to help you design your renewal page and make it available to your guests on-line. You can plan in advance, send out e-mail invitations with the address of your marriage renewal site, put up photos of your years together, and on the night of the big day, have everyone join in a live chat, perhaps even with your original priest, rabbi, or judge officiating. You can see a simple sample of photos from **Hank and Muriel Kupper's Wedding Renewal Ceremony** at http://www.tezcat.com/~jalfrank/hanmur.html. What a romantic idea!

CONCLUSION

I've covered most of the basics about how to use the computer to enhance your sex life. From sexy e-mails to chat room role-playing to virtual vow renewals, add these to your repertoire and things are sure to heat up.

Now you're ready to begin testing your sexual boundaries. We all have comfort zones around sex, but stretching them every once in a while is how we learn and grow. If you're not sure exactly how far your sexual boundaries can be pushed, the Net is a great place to try out new things and play in a safe environment. Read on for ideas about how to overcome your sexual inhibitions and find out how far you're willing to go.

ANNOTATED SITE LISTING

http://www.thriveonline.com/sex/delilah/index.html
Delilah's Nitty Gritty Sex Quiz on sexual
practices of couples in America.

http://www.gn.apc.org/inquirer/gibran.html and
gopher://gopher.ocf.berkeley.edu:70/11/
Library/Poetry/EECummings Sites of the
romantic poetry of Kahlil Gibran and e.e.
cummings.

http://www.marlo.com/card.htm and
http://www.bytesizegreetings.com/ Two on-line
card shops called Awesome Cybercard and
ByteSize Greetings.

http://www.sexycards.com/ Sexy Cards offers a
selection of x-rated virtual cards.

http://www.accelnet.com/victoria/ Victoria's Web
site contains amateur erotica by Victoria herself,
as well as lists of both real and virtual resources
for beginning writers.

http://www.persiankitty.com Persian Kitty has lists
of links to many of the finer erotic sites.

http://www.retroraunch.com Retro Raunch contains
more than 5,000 erotic photos of women and
men through the ages.

http://www.sensualsource.com/libido The Libido
site has erotic fiction, poetry, and photos of
people engaging in sexual activity.

http://www.sexuality.org/erotmass.html
Instructions for how to give an erotic massage
from the Society for Human Sexuality.

http://www.learnwell.org/~edu/connect.shtml
Learn Well Resources offers a fee-based on-line
course in relationship enhancement.

http://www.wholefamily.com/maritalcenter
The Whole Family Center offers a fee-based,
on-line, twelve-session marital-enhancement
course.

http://www.lucknet.com/personal/combo.html The
Partnership Horoscopes site explores astrological
natal charts to give you insight into your
relationship.

http://www.drruth.com Dr. Ruth's CD-ROM
encyclopedia of sex.

http://www.romdezvous.com/www45.html Adult interactive sex therapy CD-ROM.

http://www.localnet.com/~rkeinc/amore.htm Kamara Colvard's and Scott Hirni's wedding homepage.

http://www.electpress.com/loveandromance/page45.htm This part of Elect Press's site will give you ideas for writing your own wedding vows.

http://www.tezcat.com/~jalfrank/hanmur.html Hank and Muriel Kupper's on-line wedding renewal ceremony.

OVERCOMING SEXUAL INHIBITIONS

Sex is funny. Everyone knows that everyone else does it. And most of us think that everyone else is doing something different, having more fun. Yes, there's more to sex than the missionary position, but how much have you been willing to experiment? If you are willing, how do you find out where to learn new sexual techniques? (You can always try "the move" developed by Jerry Seinfeld . . . but that's the only new sexual activity they talked about for the entire run of the show!) You can use your imagination and be creative, and any sex therapist or educator you speak with will most certainly encourage this. But even if you exercise your imagination, how do you learn the technique and master the skills? Some folks watch erotic movies, but you *know* they do lots of tricks with the camera to get those shots, don't you?

If you don't have an XXX store in your town (or like most of us, you're way too embarrassed to walk in), and the thought of perusing the sexuality aisle in your neighborhood bookstore terrifies you (or you have kids and don't want to leave "those kinds of books" lying around the house), the Internet is a great place for you to learn how to expand the boundaries of your sexual repertoire. Because you can see illustrations of sexual positions and activities while you read about them, it's easy to get a good idea of what you might be willing to try and what's way out of your league. Also, you can hear about other people's experiences with those life-size sex dolls and oddly shaped toys. After you gather all the information you need, it's up to you to decide whether you want to love 'em or leave 'em.

In this chapter, I'll show you:

- The best sites to learn about new sexual techniques and positions, including enhancing your solo sex
- Where you can buy sex toys and accoutrements in the privacy of your own home
- How people use body piercings and jewelry to enhance pleasure
- Places to show off your sexual self on-line
- How to learn about the use of power and control in sexual relationships

Before we get started, you need to think about how daring you *really* are sexually. Are you satisfied with the missionary position and a sex life with no surprises? Or are you ready to embark on a mission to learn about the expansive range of sexual expression? Answer a few questions and find out:

1) If your best friend unexpectedly started talking about his or her sex life over coffee one day, you would:

___ Start choking and try hard not to spit up your drink. (1)

___ Nod enthusiastically, then change the subject. (1)

___ Ask lots of questions. (2)

___ Feel relieved, and share your own experiences. (4)

2) If a partner asked you (while undressed in the bedroom) to pretend to be something you're not, say a cashier in a grocery store or a famous astronaut, you would:

___ Say: "Sure, honey, but I'd actually rather be a rocket scientist, okay?" (4)

___ Hop to it, and get into role. (4)

___ Think he or she had totally lost his or her mind, and suggest a visit to the therapist. (1)

___ Think about it for a few minutes, fix yourself a drink, and succumb to the unknown. (2)

3) You have erotic fantasies:

___ Never. (1)

___ Only in your dreams. (2)

___ All day. (4)

___ Occasionally, when someone or something tickles your fancy. (3)

4) You have been to a sex store:
___ Once in your lifetime with a good friend as a joke. (2)
___ Never. (1)
___ Never in person, but you love to order by catalog. (4)
___ Every once in a while, when you want to spark your imagination. (4)

5) When you think about having sex with your partner, your mind wanders to:
___ Birth control and disease prevention. (2)
___ Hopes this time will be as good as the last. (4)
___ Desires of all you wish your sex life could be. (3)
___ Fear that it's that time again, and you'll have to fulfill your monthly obligation soon. (1)

6) If you had your druthers, the next time you had sex, you would:
___ Initiate something completely outrageous with your partner that you've never done before. (4)
___ Do things the way you always have. Why change something that's not broken? (2)
___ Hope your partner will think of something great to do in bed. (3)
___ Pray your partner will roll over and go to sleep before you have to actually go through with it. (1)

Add up the numbers in parentheses after the answers you selected. Here's my interpretation of your score:

6–11   You are not sexually daring in the slightest. You'd prefer to have sex only when you absolutely have to, and when you do engage, it's better if it's the same old, same old. You don't like surprises and you're not going to start liking them anytime soon. Better find other ways to make your relationship exciting, because trying new things in the bedroom is simply not your style.

12–17   You have it in you! You know there's more out there sexually, but exploring the possibilities hasn't been on the top of your priority list (you're too busy with work, the kids, keeping the house together, whatever). If your partner initiates, you're all for it, but deep down inside, you wouldn't mind coming up with some ideas of your own. It would be worth it to take the time to find out what your options are, because you might get super turned-on and have fun!

18–24   You're a sexual tiger. You have an open and inquisitive nature in all things sexual. You're the kind of person who tries all those things you see in erotic movies, even though you know they're unrealistic. Read on and get some new ideas to spur your pony—ones that are guaranteed to bring you unlimited hours of pleasure.

Now that you know whether you're a sexual daredevil, let's move on to the juicy stuff!

LEARN THE MOVES

Check this out: A group of college students (men and women) were shown the same sexually explicit video once a day for four days. Most of them were turned on the first time they saw the video. By the third day, their reactions were muted. By the fourth day, some of them were bored. On the fifth day, the researchers showed a new video—the same actors, new sexual technique. Arousal soared to just about the same level as day one.

Do human beings need variation in their lovemaking? You bet. Whether you have one partner or many, creativity in the bedroom will keep you passionate about sex. There are many ways you can add variety—positions, sex toys, location, and more (don't worry, we'll get to it all in a minute!). But one thing most couples forget to consider, according to Pat Love, the author of *Hot Monogamy*, is varying their lovemaking style. That is, changing the amount of time and effort devoted to your sexual encounters.

Love suggests having at least three distinct forms of lovemaking in your repertoire. One could be the quickie—a short, uninvolved encounter to take care of either your or your partner's needs. Another could be the standard—fifteen- to thirty-minute sessions in the bedroom with the goal of both partners having orgasms. Yet another could be the adventurous romance, where you completely change your habits and add some risk and playfulness to the sexual experience. Alternating between the three styles will remind you that there are oh, so many ways to have sex, and it most definitely doesn't have to be the same every time.

Most of us are familiar with standard lovemaking, and many of us are also adept at quickies—when we remember it's okay to have them every once in a while. But we could all use a little help with the sexual adventure. You'd be amazed at what the human body can do! And if you're in shape, creative, and flexible, you can pull off some incredible sexual feats.

In the book *Sex: A Man's Guide*, the authors cover a plethora of different sexual positions for intercourse. At one point, they put the information into an on-line database, and called it the **Position Master**. You got to choose your "desired settings" on the Position Master and then let it find the perfect position for your every need. While this may sound a bit silly, it was actually a useful tool to get new ideas and witness the incredible diversity of sexual positions.

The "settings" on the Position Master included dominant thruster (male or female), G-spot stimulation (minimum to maximum), physical rigor (minimum to maximum), ejaculatory control (minimum to maximum), and flexibility level (minimum to maximum). Here are a few examples of the positions you could get (complete with line-drawing illustrations) once you selected your desired settings:

1) Dominant Thruster	*M*
G-Spot Stimulation	*MAX*
Physical Rigor	*MAX*
Ejaculatory Control	*MAX*
Flexibility Level	*MAX*

Knees-to-Chest
This is an advanced missionary position, where the woman brings her knees to the man's chest, then wraps her legs behind his shoulders. This position allows for greater penetration while stimulating the back walls of the woman's vagina.

2) Dominant Thruster	F
G-Spot Stimulation	MAX
Physical Rigor	MAX
Ejaculatory Control	MAX
Flexibility Level	MAX

Man on Top, Woman Facing Away
In this position, the woman lies down, faceup, with her legs lifted and spread apart. The man lowers himself between her legs, facedown, with his head facing the same way as her feet. He enters her in reverse. Whoa! The drawing helps to illustrate this tricky position.

3) Dominant Thruster	F
G-Spot Stimulation	MAX
Physical Rigor	MIN
Ejaculatory Control	MAX
Flexibility Level	MIDDLE

Woman Astride, Facing Away
In this one, the woman straddles the man's body on her knees, facing the man's feet. This position allows

for deeper penetration, while giving the woman greater control.

These are just a few ideas to spur your imagination when you're surfing the Net. And they're incredibly fun to test out in real life.

BACK-DOOR MAN AND MORE

There is a community of folks on-line who are interested in giving good, solid sex information about what they call alternative sexuality, or in computer lingo, **alt.sex.** Alternative sexuality includes everything from oral and anal sex (still illegal in some states), to creative positions and fetishes. There's a newsgroup associated with this community that's gotten a little overridden the past few years with advertisements and solicitations (it's supposedly the largest newsgroup on the Net), but the FAQs (answers to frequently asked questions about a topic) are amazing (http://www.sexuality.org/1/sex/elffaq.txt). The site covers questions about male and female anatomy, sex toys, positions, anal sex, oral sex, sexually transmitted diseases, and contraception, and you can find honest answers to most of the questions about sexual variation you've thought about, but never knew whom to ask.

Some of the questions answered on the site:

- What is fellatio?
- What is "deep throating"?

- What is 69?
- Can I make my seminal fluids taste better?
- What is cunnilingus?
- How fast should I go?
- I've heard cunnilingus doesn't taste good.
- What about cunnilingus during menstruation?
- Why would anyone want to have anal sex?
- Can anal sex actually give pleasure?

Speaking of anal sex, are you one of those folks who have always thought anal sex was only for homosexual guys? A recent study of sexual practices in America found that a majority of heterosexual couples engage in anal sex as an alternative to traditional intercourse. It's the most common "kinky" sex practice in the United States.

Many people have questions and concerns about anal sex, and rightfully so, as it's one of the riskiest sexual behaviors for HIV transmission, not to mention Hepatitis B. There are a few tricks to anal sex, and if you and your partner are game, all you need to do is heed this advice:

- Make sure you are both interested in the activity.
- Use a condom (even if you are in a monogamous relationship, it's safer).
- Use lots of water-based lubricant.
- Begin by inserting a finger into the anus. It's smaller than a penis.
- Many women like to be extra relaxed before anal sex. An orgasm first helps. ;)

- If either partner wants to stop or is uncomfortable, don't think twice, just stop.

On-line, you can find out much more about anal experiences, including what to expect and how to do it at the **Anal Experience** site (http://www.ab-cybersex.com/anal_experience/default.html). This site includes FAQs (what position is best, will it hurt, is it messy, etc.). It's written in a very colloquial style, and be forewarned, there are graphic depictions of couples having anal sex. If you don't think you'll be offended, check it out, because the images are quite interesting and help to demystify the act.

PLAYING THE MAGIC FLUTE

On the other hand, while many people have curiosities or predilections toward oral sex, there are very few thoughtful, interesting sites out there at this time (most are incredibly smutty). The few I found are as follows:

THE INTERNATIONAL SOCIETY FOR THE PRACTICE OF THE ART OF CUNNILINGUS. (http://www.driveninc.com/~dogrobber/.\ispac.htm)
It sounds like a joke, but this site has some true aficionados, and some simple tips for keeping the woman in your life satisfied.

LIBERATED CHRISTIANS FILE ON FELLATIO. (http://www.sexuality.org/1/sex/libxos.txt)

One of the sources in the Society for Human Sexuality library is this file on pleasuring a man through oral sex. It is comprehensive and sensual at the same time, covering the history of the act itself, all the way through step-by-step directions on how to make your man happy.

INFO CENTER FOR SEXUAL HEALTH. (http://www.sexhealth.org/infocenter/GuideBS/oralsexintro.htm)

This site has the basics on both fellatio and cunnilingus, and addresses such concerns as: What do I do if he wants me to swallow? She doesn't taste very good, and I think it's dirty, so where do I start?

Other than these introductory sites, you can always address questions about oral sex to any of the on-line advice columnists mentioned in Chapter Three: "Explore Your Sexual Self."

None of these sites tackles the difficult question for singles: Is oral sex safe? That is, can HIV and other sexually transmitted diseases be contracted during oral activities? Most people are not particularly interested in using a condom or dental dam (latex square adapted for use to cover the vaginal lips) for oral sex. It decreases pleasure for both parties. And the sad fact is that researchers have not found conclusive evidence either way in terms of HIV transmission—that is, whether you can get the virus from performing or receiving oral sex.

One site with the latest information about disease transmission during oral sex is a part of **Thrive@Passion** called

"The Truth about Oral Sex" (http://www.thriveonline.com/
sex/oralsex.chart.html).

Developed with the help of the San Francisco Stop
AIDS project, you will find the most extensive information
on-line about the risks of both performing and receiving
oral sex for men and women. Covering diseases such as
Hepatitis B, HIV/AIDS, chlamydia, gonorrhea, and more,
the following questions are answered:

- How easy is it to get this STD through oral sex?
- What happens to someone who gets this STD?
- Can having this STD increase my risk of HIV
  infection?
- What do I need to know if my partner or I are HIV
  positive?

And the real truth about oral sex? While the jury is out
regarding HIV transmission, there are many other STDs
that can be transmitted from an infected person to their
partner during oral sex. And the scary part about STDs is
that the most common symptom is no symptom at all. So
the infected person may not know they are infected, and
pass along a virus or infection to you unknowingly.
Whether you want to take the risk with a new partner is up
to you. If you're a risk taker, then it's more important you
use condoms consistently and correctly during vaginal and
anal intercourse than oral sex. If you're not a risk taker, then
you might decide to use a condom for every exchange of
bodily fluids you have.

TABLE FOR ONE

Whether you're partnered or single, the simple fact is, masturbation is healthy. Ninety-five percent of men and over 80 percent of women have engaged or will engage in masturbation sometime in their lives. The vast majority of health and sexuality experts, from Dr. Ruth to the former Surgeon General Jocelyn Elders, agree there are no harmful side effects to solo sex. In fact, having sex with yourself has many benefits. According to Dr. Bernie Zilbergeld, author of *The New Male Sexuality*, these are just a few:

- It's fun. Why not enjoy one of the small pleasures of life?
- You don't have to look your best or concern yourself with anyone else's feelings or desires.
- It's sex with someone you love. (Okay, this one is Woody Allen's!)
- It's an excellent way to learn about how you like to be touched and stimulated.
- Masturbation is a great substitute for times when you don't have a partner, or your partner is away for a period of time.
- Mutual masturbation can be a great turn on *with* your partner.
- Used as a tool, it can help men and women overcome sexual problems (i.e. erection and premature ejaculation).

Believe it or not, there's an entire site devoted to **Solo Sex** (http://www.proaxis.com/~solo/hme.htm). Before you get to the page, there's a disclaimer that the site is dedicated to tasteful dissemination of information about human sexuality in general, masturbation in particular, so if you're offended, turn around. When you click through to the site itself, you find their motto, "Since Everybody Does 'It,' Let's Talk About 'It'!"

On the solo sex site, you'll find:

- The latest research on masturbation
- Information and articles from medical and psychological experts
- The history of masturbation
- Tips on how to improve your own self-loving
- Extensive FAQs (Will I grow hair on my palms? Is masturbation considered real sex?)
- Off-line resources
- Humor
- A personals section for people interested in sharing a masturbatory experience

Intrigued by the last item? The personal ads are mostly from men, and they want to share the experience via phone or in person. There are very few offers to exchange sexy, masturbatory e-mails. But you do have to give them credit—it's a unique idea! If you've ever thought about anonymous mutual masturbation, this is the site to find out if it's for you.

You can also find tips from other folks in this forum for new ways to masturbate. See the following advice from Mr. Mango Man:

> *Over the years I have tried many masturbation techniques. Recently I discovered that the inside of the mango skin is very slippery and intensely stimulating. I cut the skin around from top to bottom, then peel it from the fruit. I wrap it around my penis as a lining for my hand. It works wonders.*

(Beware: Some people get herpeslike sores on their skin when they touch the juices of mangoes and other tropical fruits. Folks who are allergic to mangoes should *not* try this technique!)

On a more mundane note, the FAQs from the **alt. sex.masturbation** newsgroup (http://www.sexuality.org/ 1/sex/masturba.txt/) cover the most commonly asked questions about masturbation. Examples: Can I masturbate too much? Can my partner/parent/spouse tell if I'm masturbating? There is also an extensive section on masturbatory technique for men and women. Check it out—you may pick up a few new ideas!

TOYS AREN'T JUST FOR KIDS ANYMORE

We all know it can be quite embarrassing to walk into a sex toy store, or to receive an X-rated catalog in the mail. And how do we know that? Because most of us are so timid we've never even been in one of these stores, or seen a sex catalog.

But we hear all about the variety of pleasures that can be experienced with the help of some simple sexual aids. On the Internet, you can not only purchase sex toys like vibrators, dildos, or handcuffs, you can see photographs and get complete descriptions of what each is and what it does.

It's fun just to spend some time looking at these on-line catalogs with a partner (or alone!) and imagining what you'd do to each other if you bought them. . . . Again, browsing is free—and you can browse for as long as you want in the privacy of your own home. You can also hear testimonials from other folks who have used the products, like this comment from a contented customer:

> Using the Magic Wand vibrator, I experienced a type of orgasm I have never felt before. And I've tried lots of things, believe me! I love the Wand. It's changed my life!

There are numerous sites to visit—beware, some are just fronts for pornography, but others are sincere, educational sites to help you on your way to a little more variety in the bedroom. One extensive site is **Passion Play** (http://www. cyberverse.com/~passion). "Dedicated to . . . aiding you in exploring and becoming comfortable with your own sexuality or developing intimacy with your special partner," this site is a comprehensive on-line product catalog. You can order by phone twenty-four hours a day, and shipping is said to be confidential and discreet.

The product categories include vibrators, leather, lingerie, blindfolds, nipple clamps, lubricants and other lotions, and videos. The video category includes audio cassettes and interactive videos like "Winner Takes All," an adult game of chance similar to roulette.

To take a walk on the wilder side, you can try **4SexToys**, an erotic on-line catalog (http://www.1sn.com/4sextoys). Here you can choose from an assortment of butt plugs, dildos, anal beads, vibrating vaginas, and life-size love and sex dolls. The dolls take the cake: They come in both male and female models, and the boy dolls are over 6 feet tall with vibrating penises that ejaculate when and where you tell them to. They also have a full-service suction mouth for oral pleasure. At a going rate of $149.99, these seem like a bargain. And they're disease-free!

Two of the more user-friendly on-line catalogs are **Good Vibrations** (http://www.goodvibes.com) and **Blowfish** (http://www.blowfish.com). Let's take Good Vibrations first. Started as a retail store by a sex therapist, Good Vibrations takes a woman-centered approach to healthy sexuality. They "believe that sexual pleasure is everyone's birthright, and that access to sexual materials and accurate sexual information promotes health and happiness."

You can shop for sex toys, erotica, and adult videos; tour the antique vibrator museum; or read the latest sex information and news. The toy category contains quality vibrators (electric and battery-operated), silicone toys (mostly dildos), and other sexual accessories (anal toys, harnesses, condoms, lubes, and more). The book and audio section contains selections from enlightening advice to electrifying erotica. The video section is exceptionally discriminating—each video is individually reviewed and rated. It provides a great alternative to the traditional hard-core, degrading porn so common in our culture.

If you've never seen a vibrator, the highlight of this site is the antique vibrator museum. Part of one of the original store owner's private collection, the vibrator museum will assure you that electric massagers have been in use longer than you've been alive—over 100 years! Did you know that, to this day, vibrators are marketed as massagers only, and sold in such mundane shops as pharmacies, department stores, and even the Sears catalog? In any case, the museum contains photos and descriptions of a number of recent and ancient massagers portrayed in an unintimidating way. It's worth a look.

The Blowfish Catalog (http://www.blowfish.com) is the oldest on-line catalog of sex toys and accoutrements. Their motto is simple: "Good products for great sex." Also committed to sex education and positive sexuality, the site includes Fishnet, an on-line sex magazine. Complete with a question-and-answer column by a sex therapist, erotic fiction, and essays, the magazine is up-to-date and engaging.

The catalog contains the standards: sex toys, supplies, and books, but the clincher sections are the objets d'art, comics, and the videos. In the objets d'art section, you'll find such oddities as erotic needlepoints, vulva hand pup-pets, breast and penis jewelry, and bumper stickers. The comics section has an unusual selection of well-drawn, un-derground adult comic books. And the extensive video se-lection is arranged by title, as well as by topic. You'll find diverse titles under subtopics such as Chick Flicks, Slapstick, Costume Dramas, High Gloss, and Cinema Verité. It's easy to shop here, with confidentiality guaranteed.

And don't forget **Condomania** on-line (http://www.condomania.com). Condomania was America's first condom boutique, opened in New York City in 1991. Now there are two stores, in NYC and LA, with more planned in the future. The idea behind both the on-line store and the real-life ones is to create a hip, fun, G-rated, relaxed environment to promote safe sex and condom use. The Web site is chock-full of five hundred pages of safer sex info, including an on-line catalog of over two hundred products. The coolest part of the site is the Condom Wizard, an interactive condom search guide. You tell the Condom Wizard what you're looking for in a condom (sensitivity, size, texture, flavor, lubrication, latex, strength), answer another question or two, and get back a listing of between one and ten choices (complete with descriptions and order form) that meet your needs and desires. Sure makes staring at the drugstore rack look outdated!

STICK IT TO ME

As we approach the end of the '90s, we are faced with an amazing amount of body art. From piercings to scarification to tattoos and branding, even mainstream folks are taking a walk on the wild side. Body art is considered sexy by some, but it's only piercings that are valued for their increased sexual sensitivity. If you've ever considered the possibility of getting a new hole (or your teenager has threatened you with it!), the Web is a great place to get all the facts you need to make an informed decision.

Turns out there are many, many different types of genital piercings. For women, the hood of the clitoris is more commonly pierced than the clitoris itself because the procedure is less complicated and safer. It takes the skin approximately one to two months to heal after the piercing is done. Women can also pierce their outer labia, inner labia, outer labia to their inner labia, the triangle between the clitoris and labia, the mons to the outer labia—the alternatives are exhausting.

Men most often pierce their penises, although it's also possible to pierce the scrotum for extrasensory stimulation. Penis piercings can be horizontal or vertical through the head of the penis, through the foreskin, on the shaft, at the base of the scrotum, or through the perineum (the area of skin between the scrotum and the anus). There is no evidence of penis piercings causing urinary tract infections in either sexual partner. For more details on all aspects of piercings, including nipple pierces, see the extensive **FAQs about piercings** at http://www.cs.ruu.nl/wais/html/nadir/bodyart/piercing-faq/jewelry/.html.

You can also find some good discussion about the pros and cons of piercing and body art at **Flesh Canvas** (http://www.fleshcanvas.com/main.htm), a monthly online tattoo and body piercing mag. If you're considering a genital pierce, you can post a message on this site to get info and advice. Like most messages in this forum, this man included an e-mail address to send replies:

> *I'm considering a penis piercing and would like some*
> *advice from those of you who have them as to which*
> *of the options provides the most sexual enhancement*
> *(for both me and the wife). My wife is very conserva-*
> *tive and will probably go bonkers when I mention it.*
> *Any advice on how to approach the subject? Also, any*
> *recommendations on shops in the Dayton, OH, area?*
> *Thanks in advance.*

If the idea of piercing your genitals makes you queasy, or you'd rather try something similar to see if it really does enhance the sexual experience before you make a commitment, check out **Body Jewelry by Judy** (http://www.sexy-jewelry.com/). You can see photos of "models posing while erotically adorned with stimulating, non-piercing body jewelry designed to look beautiful, feel incredible, and inspire passion." Their bestsellers are available on-line, and include the gamut of clit clips and titty twinklers for women, frenulum (the sensitive spot on the underside tip of the penis) ticklers for men, and burn baubles for both genders (attach near the anus).

What is she talking about? Okay, here's the deal. Clit clips are adjustable, comfortable clips that slip over the clitoris easily and painlessly, creating wonderful stimulation and delicate visual effect. The frenulum ticklers slip loosely behind the head of the penis, and are held snugly in place against the frenulum, providing stimulus and decoration at the same time. If you're not convinced, visit the site and check it out (twenty-one years and older only, on the honor system).

TAKE IT OFF (OR WATCH!)

Have you ever walked in front of your window naked or semidressed, only to find someone watching you? Were you aroused at the prospect? When you were in college, did you ever walk in on your roommate having sex, and stand silently watching for a while? Have you ever listened to your neighbors doing it, and secretly enjoyed the experience? Or had sex with your partner as loud as you could because you knew someone else was listening and getting off? If the answer is yes to any of these questions, the Internet is a great place for you to explore the "fetish" of exhibitionism/voyeurism. You can show off your body (or your partner's or friend's) in an anonymous environment and see what kinds of reactions you get. Safe, secure, and potentially titillating . . .

The first place you might like to visit in order to decide if virtual exhibitionism is for you is the **Shy Exhibitionist** (http://www.shyx.com/shy2.shtml). This site was built by a woman who realized she was an exhibitionist after she posted some photos on a newsgroup and was turned on by the racy responses. She asks you these questions: "Do you enjoy getting those knowing looks when you're dressed sexy? Does your lover enjoy showing you off? Maybe you're wondering what it's like to hear from people who've seen your picture on the Web?" For $9.95 a month, you get a monthly Shy Exhibitionist cyberzine, complete with photographs and stories chronicling public exposure. The Shy Exhibitionist will also pay *you* $250.00 if she publishes your erotic photo, so this is a good place to have a chance at it.

If you're still wondering what the thrill is, here's an excerpt from the Shy Exhibitionist's postings in a newsgroup forum on the Web. This was posted complete with photos of her that become increasingly revealing as you scroll down the page:

I was really surprised and delighted by all the positive responses I received to my last posting. . . . Some were very explicit. At first, it really threw me for a loop and I didn't know how to react. As time went on, and I received more like them, it made me feel very desirable and excited. I started to look forward to receiving your mail.

I really never thought I was pretty or sexy, and you've given me a lot of self-confidence. With that in mind, I felt a little more daring to go one step further.

These shots were taken at a local park. Even though you can't SEE anyone, there were men strolling by and others playing basketball. It didn't take long for a few to notice what was going on. During the time I had my blouse undone, there were a couple of guys playing football. They kept throwing the ball closer and closer to me. I'm sure they got an eyeful. I enjoyed that.

Another site devoted to exhibitionism, although a bit more amateurish, is **Clay's Page of Exhibitionism** (http://www. freebeer.com/clay/ClaysPage.htm). Clay operates a scanning service on-line, so you can drop him a note if you want to see yourself, or your lover, wife, or friend on the Net. He'll scan and post your images for you so others can view them at their leisure. One of the featured photos when I visited the site was Cindy, a self-professed happily married mother of two, who loves to flash in malls (and wherever else) for both men and women. There are also amateur stories of public exhibitionism on the site with titles like Viva Las Vegas, Public Orgasm, DT's Club, and New Deck.

On the other side of the coin, there's the **Voyeur's Playground** (http://www.voyeurplay.inter.net). This site is the home of The Voyeur, an on-line newsletter; amateur hidden camera photos and movies of people in various stages of undress; and a resource list of where to buy equipment to be a voyeur in real life. A little scary, but hey, if it's out there, someone gets aroused by it, right?

FETISHISM

Speaking of festishes, the Web is home to the **Fetish Resource Guide** (http://www.viaverde.com/sex/fetish.htm). This site is a listing of links on all the major sexual fetish topics including big people, body art, bodybuilders, boots, corsets, costumes, feet, smoking, spanking, uniforms, vampires, and more. If you think you might be interested, this is the site to get you started. It's well organized, and has a very short download time.

Here's the dirt on fetishes: A fetish is an inanimate object thought to have magical or healing powers. A sexual fetish is an object thought to have sexual power, and because of this becomes the center of a person's erotic interest and satisfaction. Sexual excitement is triggered by the object or particular trait, not by the person who is wearing the object or who has the trait.

Fetishes can be a very powerful sexual turn-on. The key to keeping a fetish in the normal range is to make sure you don't *need* the object in order to get turned on. For example, if you get aroused when your wife is wearing a rubber catsuit, that's normal. But if you need her to be in a catsuit in order to get turned on, you're delving into the world of hard-core fetishism.

It's hard to know what you might like sexually, although many of us have latent turn-ons we'd like to explore. To get some ideas, and to judge whether your turn-on is normal or fetishistic, you can check some of the on-line forums, like the Turn Ons, Turn Offs board at **Thrive@Passion** (http://www.thriveonline.com/passion.html). Here are what some of the men and women are saying:

> *I can't help it . . . I just love a man in uniform. Be it army, police . . . whatever. I love a disciplined man and a man in uniform has discipline.*

> *I love circumcised men. It really gets me hot and bothered when they are hot, hard, cut, and horny. Hee, hee, hee!*

> *I hate it when women want me to jump off the wardrobe, do a somersault, and land between their legs.*

I am a 39-year-old, average-looking male, seeking any females who love to have their feet worshiped . . . I love to kiss, suck, smell, & lick female feet. I also give pedicures.

If it's out there, it's on the Web. And you can explore to your heart's content, without making a commitment. If you find something that sounds interesting, you can take it home and try it on for size!

THE POWER PLAY

The success of any relationship depends on managing the dynamics of power and control. Like it or not, when two people get together, for a short time or the long haul, you've got to balance your own needs with your partner's, and that means dealing with power.

While most of us limit our struggles to lovers' quarrels and decisions about which restaurant to eat at, some couples (and singles) have decided to look more intensely at their power and control dynamics in the form of the BDSM (bondage, domination, sadism, masochism) sexual experience.

According to the **Power Politics** site (http://www. bdsm.com/powerotics/home.htm), "erotic power exchange is any situation where partners, of their own free will and choice, actively and willfully incorporate the power element into their lovemaking. Also known as BDSM, S&M, D/s, or sadomasochism, erotic power exchange is informed, consensual, safe, sane and voluntary. The acts involved range from using blindfolds during sex to 24/7 dedication or branding."

Power Politics is the largest nonprofit electronic magazine about erotic power exchange dedicated to heterosexual dominant men and submissive women. The site contains general, useful information to help beginners understand the concept behind erotic power exchange as well as providing a place for veterans to meet and converse about their experiences.

This site has three sections: the Public Dungeon (the part of the site available to all who visit), the "Pay Per View" section, and the members-only Private Dungeon. There is also a gothic-oriented cosite, La Société Libertaine. A Powerotics membership includes things like unlimited access to over 250 pages in addition to the public section, talking to others in discussion groups and virtual cafés, exclusive interviews with real doms and submissives, expert answers to your questions, discounts on other sites, lots more pictures and artwork, and info on how to make your own inexpensive toys and gear.

In the Public Dungeon (that's the free area), you can find general information about erotic power exchange, including:

- What it is
- FAQ (covering control, taboos, roles in real life, scenes, fetishes, and more)
- Information for professionals
- Truth and prejudice

- Stages of getting involved in erotic power exchange
- Legalities
- Libraries
- Erotic power exchange and relationships
- How to play fun scenes
- Safe play and safe sex

Testimonies like the following two abound in the public forum, making it easier for newbies to get involved with the membership:

I am very excited to see what the Internet has done for the BDSM scene. Living in the Midwest (USA) it is hard to meet people with similar interests. Thanks to sites like this I can network with others with similar tastes and not feel like a freak.

I'm 30 now and have played lightly before (role-playing). I remember having been really turned on by lingerie when I was 11 or 12. My ex-girlfriends have all been fairly vanilla. I came close to marrying one of them once. For her birthday, I bought her a complete outfit (stockings, garters, bra, panties, and teddy), but she was embarrassed! We broke up a year later (it took a while) and I totally immersed myself in my career. I've only recently "outed" to myself that yes, I have fetishes, I am a dom at heart, and I will pursue these interests. I've also brought myself to where I can say I don't care what anybody thinks of what I'm doing 'cause it's my life and what I want to do! (And it isn't sick, perverse, or any number of things people who don't understand the scene may think). But yes, in a lot of instances I suppressed those feelings because I was shy and afraid of peer pressure. Society is still very puritanical!

La Société Libertaine is a Goth site that contains a number of erotic stories of domination and submission, along with technical advice and information about related fetishes, including cages and confinement, edge play, Japanese bondage, water sports, chastity belts, and food play. The Society sponsors a number of partner facilities for BDSM practice, as well as exclusive in-person power erotic events and gatherings around the country.

To join the club, it costs $25.00 a year for Powerotics alone, and $50.00 for both Powerotics and Libertaine. You can also go for broke and pay $7.50 for temporary access to a substantial part of the member information, including the picture gallery, fiction and poetry, advanced safety guide, make-your-own-toy section, and the partner search profiles. The $7.50 fee is for one access that lasts until the next Saturday at midnight, meaning it could be for one day or seven, depending on when you pay your fee.

What's interesting about this site is that it supports both on-line BDSM relationships and off-line ones. For those looking to try out roles on-line, there are people to meet, chat rooms to congregate in, and forums in which to post and read. For those in real-life erotic power relationships, there are separate areas for both doms and submissives where people talk about and negotiate their experiences.

One area of the site is specifically for women in real-life submissive relationships. It's called Latches, and current topics under discussion on their mailing list, in their chat rooms, and other venues include:

- Dealing with children in the household
- Dangerous dominants
- Dominants who deceive you
- Living a dual life (about those with spouses or significant others who have no interest in D&S)
- Finding balance and equilibrium while living as a submissive
- Does a submissive in an absolute power-exchange relationship have the freedom to leave?
- Growing up in a D&S household
- In and out of the bedroom
- The importance of physical appearance
- Punishment

The list of topics is a lot longer. What makes these discussions different from others is that they involve painfully honest and very real portrayals of the struggles, successes, and failures of living within a power-exchange relationship. Much of the abstract theory and rhetoric so common in kinky discussion groups is gone and we are left with the voices of real experience. Here's an excerpt from one of the essays of a member of Latches:

Like so many of you, I first became aware of "the scene" on-line. A friend from a vanilla (not BDSM) channel convinced me to go to a D/s channel with him. Frankly, I was a bit curious, but nothing more. However, once there, I began to ask some questions and I found that something inside of me awoke. It felt right. Even more strange was that I seemed to fall into the submissive role naturally. The strange part was that I am, in many respects, a forceful, pushy, aggressive, opinionated, too often smart-assed kind of person. I am also intelligent, educated, with an appreciation for many different kinds of art, music, literature, etc. In other words, I am a person who is quite capable of making decisions and managing my own life.

How do you begin to get involved with these sites? Try signing up for a $7.50 access so you can get the full flavor of the area. If you've ever found the thought of being bound during sex a turn-on, or you've had fantasies of being forced to have sex (very common for more women than you might imagine), or if you like the idea of giving up your power (or taking your power) in the bedroom, this site is a safe place to play and explore your fantasies. Be aware, though, when on this particular site, do *not* click on the photos or ads on the first few pages. They are advertisements that will take you to paying sites with incredibly long download times, and they do not provide the safe environment that a site like Powerotics does.

While most BDSM heterosexual relationships have men in the dominant role with a submissive female counterpart, there is a subculture of dominant women and sub-

missive men. Take a look at the **Frugal Domme** (http://
www.frugaldomme.com). This site is mostly a catalog of
inexpensive products for BDSM use, but it also includes
good information about technique and scene ideas, etiquette tips, dangers and precautions, home manufacturing
techniques, and an Ask Domina advice column. Here's a
sample of the questions that Domina answers:

> *Dear Domina,*
> *I tried to tell my dom my limits on our first meeting,*
> *and she told me that if I were truly submissive, I'd do*
> *whatever she wished. Should I be assertive about*
> *things I won't do, or would that mean I'm not really a*
> *sub? Some things she wants me to do make me very*
> *upset.*
> *—Teddy*

> *Dear Teddy,*
> *Negotiations should be from the standpoint of equals.*
> *You don't negotiate "en role." Just because you are a*
> *sub does not mean the dom should set your limits for*
> *you or deny you the right to set limits. Of course you*
> *should have limits, and if a dom respects you, she will*
> *respect your limits. If you don't set limits, you may*
> *suddenly find yourself tied up and being sliced with-*
> *out realizing how you got there.*

> *D/s is supposed to be safe, sane, and consensual. Con-*
> *sensual means that both parties have the right to*
> *choose. . . . No one should be doing things that upset*

them emotionally or are physically impossible. You have the right to say no to anything. And your dom has the duty to help you find your limits and to respect your limits.

You have the responsibility to help your dom find your limits, and to trust her to help you to stretch limits. Your limits will change over time, but some limits will remain constant. . . . Your negotiation will remain constant all during your relationship. Limits will change. But you need to set limits and keep setting them.
—Domina

If this all seems a bit too much, you might want to check out the on-line companion to Gloria Brame's book, **Different Loving** (http://www.gloria-brame.com/diflove.htm). It includes an excellent library of erotic power poetry and fiction, interviews on various kinks, an Ask Gloria advice column, and a graphics gallery. Samples from Gloria's personal erotica follows:

When you meet me, you will be dressed exactly as follows. First, no underwear, of any kind. Over your bare chest, you are to wear a shirt which buttons down the front so I can open it and reach in to squeeze and pinch your nipples whenever I please. Over your bare rear, you will wear your tightest, thinnest pair of pants, pants which fit so snugly over your crotch that everything is visible at a glance. . . . I will enjoy rub-

*bing my hand over your crotch, even more so when
you involuntarily respond to my rough caresses with
moans of desire.*

*If you are good and don't question me, I will allow
you to wear a long jacket over the pants—but only
while you are traveling to meet me. The moment you
arrive at the spot I've designated, you must remove
it and wait . . . so that you are on display when I
approach. . . .*

*You will have to wait with your hands clasped behind
your back and your head bowed, and you will not
speak, under any circumstances. You will stand like
that until I arrive and release you from this frozen,
silent pose. . . .*

Perhaps most impressive on the Different Loving site are
the Kinks Links, which catalog over 1,400 handpicked links
to S&M fetish sites on the Web. With categories like the
ABCs of D&S, home pages of kinky people on the Net,
bondage, spanking, body modification, fetishes, scene zines,
kinky fiction, and safe sex, these links cover the gamut of
possibilities. It's a good place to explore, see what turns you
on, and which lines you're willing to cross. If nothing else,
you will expand your knowledge of the range of sexual activities possible, making you more open to experimenting
in the bedroom.

CONCLUSION

If you haven't overcome your inhibitions just by reading the descriptions of various sexual possibilities, then you had better turn on your computer and start surfing. Because if there's a sexual activity out there, any kind of sexual turn-on, you can find someone who's thought of it on the Net.

Don't get the idea that you have to run out and tie up your next blind date, or insist your wife have anal sex repeatedly for the next month. Be cool. Remember that change is difficult for most of us, and we all have our limits of what we're willing to engage in sexually. What you've gained from this chapter is the simple fact of knowing all these sexual variations exist, and that makes you more open as a human being to the range of sexual possibilities.

Now it's time to take a peek at some lesser-known sexual activities. In the next chapter, "Beyond the Picket Fence," I'll help you open your eyes to sexual possibilities you may have heard of, but never gave a second thought.

Turns out that you can learn about cyberswinging, swapping, gender-bending, and more, all in the relative safety of your own computer-enabled home. Opening your mind to these sexual possibilities may surprise you—people you know and always thought of as "normal" may turn out to be more interesting than you had imagined.

ANNOTATED SITE LISTING

http://www.sexuality.org/1/sex/elffaq.txt FAQs for
the alternative sexuality newsgroup.

**http://www.ab-cybersex.com/anal_experience/
default.html** The Anal Experience site tells you
what to expect and how to participate in anal
sex play.

http://www.driveninc.com/~dogrobber/.\ispac.htm
The International Society for the Practice of the
Art of Cunnilingus has simple tips for keeping
the woman in your life satisfied.

http://www.sexuality.org/1/sex/libxos.txt Liberated
Christians File on Fellatio is a comprehensive
and sensual guide to pleasuring a man through
oral sex.

**http://www.sexhealth.org/infocenter/GuideBS/
oralsexintro.htm** The Info Center for Sexual
Health has the basics on both fellatio and
cunnilingus.

**http://www.thriveonline.com/sex/
oralsex.chart.html** Thrive@Passion's "Truth
about Oral Sex" provides extensive information
about the STD risks of both performing and
receiving oral sex on men and women.

http://www.proaxis.com/~solo/hme.htm Solo Sex is
a site devoted to the celebration of masturbation.

http://www.sexuality.org/1/sex/masturba.txt FAQs
from the alt.sex.masturbation newsgroup cover
the most commonly asked questions about

masturbation, and provide techniques for both
men and women.

http://www.cyberverse.com/~passion Passion Play
is a comprehensive on-line sex toy catalog.

http://www.1sn.com/4sextoys 4SexToys is a wilder
erotic on-line catalog that includes products such
as life-size love and sex dolls.

http://www.goodvibes.com At Good Vibrations, you
can shop for sex toys, brush up on the latest sex
news, or visit the antique vibrator museum.

http://www.blowfish.com The Blowfish Catalog is
the oldest on-line catalog of sex toys and
accoutrements.

http://www.condomania.com Condomania is an on-
line condom boutique, featuring the Condom
Wizard to help you make your selection.

**http://www.cs.ruu.nl/wais/html/na-dir/bodyart/
piercing-faq/jewelry/. html** These FAQs provide
details on all aspects of body piercing.

http://www.sexy-jewelry.com/ Body Jewelry by Judy
is a catalog of sexual jewelry you can wear
without being pierced.

http://www.fleshcanvas.com/main.htm Flesh
Canvas is a monthly on-line tattoo and body
piercing mag.

http://www.shyx.com/shy2.shtml The Shy
Exhibitionist is a cyberzine of stories and
chronicles of public exposure.

http://www.freebeer.com/clay/ClaysPage.htm Clay's
Page of Exhibitionism will scan and post your

erotic images of yourself for others' viewing pleasure.

http://www.voyeurplay.inter.net Voyeur's Playground is an on-line newsletter containing amateur hidden-camera pictures and movies of men and women in various stages of undress.

http://www.viaverde.com/sex/fetish.htm Fetish Resource Guide is a list of links to all the major sexual fetish topics.

http://www.bdsm.com/powerotics/home.htm The Power Politics site is devoted to erotic power exchange between heterosexual dominant men and submissive women.

http://www.frugaldomme.com Frugal Domme is a catalog of inexpensive products for BDSM use.

http://www.gloria-brame.com/diflove.htm The Different Loving site includes an excellent library of erotic power poetry and fiction, as well as Kinks Links to other BDSM sites on the Web.

CHAPTER SEVEN

BEYOND THE PICKET FENCE

You've read the book so far, and you're saying, been there, done that. What else has she got to say? What can top it off? Really . . . you've practiced your flirting skills, found love, gotten your sex advice, heightened your fantasies, spiced up your relationship, explored new activities, and now you're ready for more. Okay, make sure you're sitting down for this one.

I know I've said you can find anything and everything on-line. And it's true. So now we're going to go over the top. Take a walk on the wild side. Swapping and swinging, gender-bending, future sex . . . Ever wonder about these things? How do people who have more than one mate pull it off? What is it like to be a man trapped in a woman's body? Or to feel good dressing in women's clothing? And as for the future of sex, what do you really think it will be like?

Can you help shape what's to come? It's the '90s and you can explore the possibilities, join a chat, or find information and support for a lifestyle you've heard about, but have no clue as to what it is.

The Net is the place to find out what other people do behind closed doors . . . to open your mind to all kinds of possibilities. I'm not suggesting everyone become polyamorous or a cross-dresser, but I do believe we need to learn about other options in order to stay objective. Being judgmental closes us up—it shuts down sexual expressiveness. Once you get beyond ignorance and open your mind and heart to the variations, you'll be pleasantly surprised. You'll begin to realize some people you know are cross-dressers, others share partners, and still others are defining the future of sexuality as we know it. If you don't allow the possibilities to exist, you'll never learn these things about the people you know and love. And you'll spend too much time in ignorance of the expanse of sexual expression.

In this chapter, I'll cover:

- Alternatives to monogamy: What they are, where to find support on the Net
- Gender-bending: Definitions, information, on-line services, and community
- The future of sex: Predictions and virtual resources to keep you up-to-the-minute as the millennium approaches.

Before we get started, I want you to think about the future of sex yourself. Let your imagination run wild, test its strength to see how far you can stretch the boundaries. Answer the following questions, but this time, put your answers in writing and send them to me. We'll define the future of sex together. Who better than you and your friends reading this book? You can contact me via e-mail at DebLevine@hotmail.com, or snail mail at P.O. Box 190663, San Francisco, CA 94119-0663 USA.

1) Will our society be more sexually adventurous in the new millennium, or less?

2) Will it be acceptable to have more than one spouse or partner at once?

3) Will we encounter more or less divorce in our society?

4) Do you think someone will invent sexbots—robots that can take the place of a live person for the purposes of sex?

5) Will conversation about sex and sexuality become more commonplace in our culture, or less?

6) Will information about sex be more or less readily available?

7) Will there be a time in the new millennium when the entire range of sexual expression will be accepted?

8) Do you think sex will be viewed as a health issue or continue as a lifestyle/social concern? Or will it be put into a third category altogether?

9) Will virtual-reality sex—computer simulations— become commonplace as we start to rely on computers for everything?

10) What other forms of cybersex do you think might emerge after the year 2000?

11) Will these changes affect only U.S. society and culture, or will there be international implications as well?

12) How do you think your personal sex life will change in the new millennium?

Be as exhaustive as you like in your answers. And be on the lookout for my next book. . . .

Okay, now let's review what's out there in cyberspace today. Ready, set, go!

ALTERNATIVES TO MONOGAMY

A couple hundred years ago, talking about "open sexual relationships" might have gotten you tried as a witch. Not much has changed, except possibly that curiosity has replaced moral outrage. These days, if you meet someone in an open relationship, the burning question would most likely be, "How do you manage without getting jealous?"

"Polyamory" literally means loving more than one. Some polyamorous couples engage in outside sex as a couple; others have individual sexual ventures. Some heterosexual couples invite only one man at a time to join them; others are more involved with women. No matter the derivative, advocates of polyamory emphasize open lines of communication, honesty, and agreement on rules between members of the primary couple.

The **Open Hearts Project** (http://world.std.com/ ~bearpaw/ohp.html) collects advice for polyamorous couples who want to successfully avoid misunderstanding and jealousy. Here are some of their general guidelines:

> **I will play safe.** If adhered to, this removes one of the main worries about open relationships, the possibility of sexually transmitted diseases and pregnancy.
>
> **Tell me about it.** Partners must tell each other about outside involvement, ideally beforehand.
>
> **Don't tell me about it.** Partners don't want to hear about outside liaisons. Out of sight is out of mind for these folks.
>
> **The veto.** Partners need to have prior and ongoing approval of a given outside involvement.
>
> **Sex only.** It's okay to have sex outside the relationship but not to get emotionally involved.
>
> **Only together.** It's okay to have an outside involvement, as long as both partners are involved with the third party.

Each of these is an agreement on its own, or can be combined in various formats. Note that agreements do not have to be symmetrical—for example, one person in a relationship could decide not to get sexually involved outside the relationship, but still give permission for his or her partner to become involved with someone new.

I don't know why I prefer being polyamorous. It's certainly more complicated. It's not as safe, emotionally or physically (safer sex notwithstanding). It's definitely less accepted.

I know that with certain friends, I really enjoy being physical. The conscious, deliberate agreements I have with my primary partner set the limits for each of my outside relationships, and it works for us.

You can find a basic introduction to polyamory, or responsible nonmonogamy, on the Open Hearts site, along with the guidelines set out above. There is also a small collection of autobiographical stories by and about polyamorous relationships. You can contribute your own and see it posted on-line if you like. The Project is looking for practicalities (this is how we do it) and feelings (this is how I (we) feel about what we do).

The benefits of an open relationship include being able to follow through on outside attractions, the removal of fear of illicit affairs, and a stress release for any buildup in a long-term closed relationship. As long as the sex is safe and mutual, advocates of open relationships wouldn't have it any other way.

You love each other. Your sex life is wonderful. And yet . . . you spend long hours together, discussing, deciding, wondering if this is really what you want, knowing it's a life-changing decision. We were all brought up in a monogamous world and taught we belong exclusively to the one we love. Taught that sex, while pleasurable, is reserved for the marriage bed. And part of this statement is true. We do belong only to each other, in many respects. So why are we looking for more? The answer is that everyone, whether they admit it to themselves or not, fantasizes about having sex with someone other than their spouse. Those of us who can be honest with ourselves and share that honesty with our partner are more able to make the fantasy become a reality, based on a solid relationship we have with our mates. We are the people who realize the difference between making love and having sex. And we are the people who realize the joys of sharing each other sexually.

The **Lifestyles** site (http://www.playcouples.com) is also dedicated to polyamory and has an extensive community of sensuous adult couples who want to explore their sexuality to the fullest. In former times, these folks would have been called swingers—a subculture of people who enjoy being sexual with acquaintances and friends. These days, many equate the term *swingers* with irresponsibility, and the Lifestyles group is anything but irresponsible. It is a very sophisticated group that gets together in real life around the country, provides exotic travel tours for members, chat rooms and forums for discussions of swinging, and personal ads to meet others of like mind.

We have recently entered into this "couples" dating, as I prefer to call it, and have found it very exciting. It has actually enhanced our marriage and opened up a whole new world for us. I am learning new things about my wife and she is learning more about me. Obviously not for everyone—don't even consider doing this unless you have a STRONG trustful relationship to begin with. I was a very jealous man at one point. . . . I am now leaving jealousy behind . . . and building a very strong marriage . . . into an even stronger one. Cheating on spouses is a major cause of ruined relationships. I no longer have the desire to cheat . . . there is no need . . . :)

The Lifestyles motto is "freedom of sexual expression and tolerance towards the private lives of others." It is definitely a couples club, and with a $20.00 a year membership, you get a $15.00 discount on the annual convention fees, $15.00 off any Lifestyles travel tour, mailings, the *Lifestyles Journal*, and free personal-ad publication on- and off-line. On-line chat costs an extra $10.00 a month, or $25.00 for three months for members only.

Another site devoted to exploring alternatives to monogamy is the **Loving More** site (http://www.lovemore.com/). This site includes articles like "How to Have a Successful Non-Monogamous Relationship," "At the Heart of Jealousy," and "Threesomes—Make it Last." There is a section for polyamorous news and events, an e-mail discussion group, chat, message boards, links, and personal ads. I must admit that on a Saturday afternoon, there was only one person chatting, so the chat part of the site has yet to take off. The message boards have some good dialogue about locating groups interested in polyamory, and support for making your polyamorous relationship work.

Members of Loving More ($49.00 a year at the time of writing) get access to extra forums, free personal ads, four issues of the *Loving More* magazine, and on-line conferencing and referrals. To receive the magazine only, it costs $24.00 a year.

You can also find a thriving community of polyamory advocates at the home page for the Usenet newsgroup, **alt.polyamory** (http://www.polyamory.org). This site includes FAQs about the newsgroup, articles on common mistakes made in polyamorous relationships, events, mailing lists, Web sites of some polyamorous folks, and poly-personals. The newsgroup itself is a fairly sophisticated forum for discussion and support of the polyamorous lifestyle. It includes topics like how to explain your situation to your monogamous friends and family, tips and advice for bringing up the idea of polyamory with a partner, and how to tell if you're polyamorous. There is also a companion newsgroup called **alt.personals.poly** where you can post and read polyamorous personal ads. As with all newsgroups, this site is free and highly trafficked.

If your partner is not as enthusiastic as you are about polyamory, sharing a threesome fantasy during sex can give you both an idea of whether it might be exciting. There are too many in this lifestyle who are in it to please their partner rather than themselves. That's a mistake. Let your partner know that you don't want her participating just to please you—that you genuinely want to understand her feelings on the idea; she'll be more comfortable filling you in truthfully. If you are able to communicate at this level, without attempting to manipulate each other, that in itself is a major accomplishment most monogamous couples never attain.

Lastly, there's a site where you can find a list of people interested in polyamory with their on-line contact information at the **Polyamory—North America** site (http://www.sonic.net/naturat/poly/poly.html). This site includes a matrix of people's names, e-mail addresses, ICQ numbers (this is an Internet service that allows for private chatting and searches for your friends on-line and alerts you when they sign on), remarks (seeking BiMs and couples in the South), languages spoken, and geographic area. This site provides a great way to talk to polyamorous folks and find out about their lifestyle choices.

GENDER-BENDING

Have you ever stared at a beautiful woman, only to realize after a time that she's a he? Did you see the movie *The Crying Game*? How about *Victor, Victoria*? Or maybe you once caught your kid brother dressing up in Mom's clothing? Most of us have experienced an instance or two where we've seen a man dress in women's clothes or affect feminine traits. But most of us have no clue as to why.

> *I got caught once many, many years ago. I was a junior in high school and got home from school hours before anyone else. I used this time to experiment and*

try on my mother's and sister's clothing. I had just gotten all dressed up in my sister's minidress, stockings, and heels when I heard a key in the front door. I ran into the bathroom just as my dad walked in the door. I thought I could grab something out of the hamper to wear and ditch the other clothes there. But when I opened it, the hamper was empty. My dad knocked on the door and asked me what was going on. I had no choice but to come out. Was he ever surprised! He asked me what I was doing and all I could say was "trying on some of Mom's and Sis's clothes." He then asked if I could control what I was doing, to which I answered, "Yes." "Good," he said. "Then don't do it anymore." He told me that he would get help if I couldn't control it, and that was the last word he ever said on the subject.

Let's get our terms straight before we go any further:

Cross-dressers. Heterosexuals who occasionally wear clothing of the opposite gender

Transvestites. People who dress to look like the opposite gender full-time

Transsexuals. People who believe they were born into the wrong-gender body and often try to change it medically

Intersexed people. Those who were born with chromosomal or hormonal defects causing them not to fit into standard male and female gender categories

Sexual orientation. Which sex you find sexually
   attractive
Sexual identity. How you see yourself physically
Gender identity. How you see yourself socially

Believe it or not, there are over two million heterosexual
cross-dressers in the United States alone. These men do not
want to become women, they simply desire to emulate them.
According to **Tri-Ess** (http://www.tri-ess.com/), an organization for hetero cross-dressers, their spouses and significant others, and their families, "so great is a crossdresser's
admiration and respect for women that they seek to identify with them in an effort to feel their own womanliness."

> *Hi, I'm a little nervous, but here goes. . . . I'm 42,
> married to a wonderful woman with two beautiful
> children. I love to cross-dress and sometimes dream of
> being a woman. No one knows about this at all, be-
> cause I want it that way. I wouldn't think of jeopar-
> dizing the family I love.*

Adult male heterosexual cross-dressers do not do it for
money—those are female impersonators. The Tri-Ess site
provides a place on-line for discussion and support of
cross-dressing and its effect on your personal life. You can
get a fair amount of information on the public part of the
Web site, and if you join, for $25.00 a year you get quarterly
publications of the Femme Mirror, a national members' directory with a blind e-mail service, and access to the complete Web site with forums, personal ads, and chat rooms.

You have to send your name and/or femme name, mailing address, or e-mail address in order to request an application. In addition, you must pledge confidentiality of the membership, as well as the fact that you *are* a cross-dresser in order to join.

Another informative site about gender-bending is **The Online Gender Support Group** (http://www.gendertalk. com). This area offers information and resources ranging from makeup secrets to hormones to stories about getting caught cross-dressing. You can find answers to your questions about how gender issues relate to spirituality, dating, transsexualism, and more. There is a gender news service, links, and an information center. The highlight of this site, though, is the "live" radio show, GenderTalk. Broadcast once a week from Boston, then archived on the Web, this is "the only worldwide program that talks about transgenderism in the first person." You can hear exciting new voices on the show that challenge our traditional view of gender. Each program runs from forty-five minutes to an hour long, and you need RealAudio in order to listen. If you don't have it, there is a link to the site where you can download the software for free.

Once you get to the list of transcripts, you'll find topics such as Transgender Medicine, Trans Humor, The Finishing School for Boys Who Want to Be Girls, Politics and Art, and Transgender Sexuality. The shows themselves are witty and quick-paced. The two hosts are excellent. You need a 28.8 or 14.4 modem to get the show, and the only thing that comes off as odd is listening to people with women's names speak in men's voices. The detriments of radio, but at least you don't get distracted by how the trans-gendered folks look!

This site also has an IRC channel for discussion of transgender issues. It's #crossdress on EFnet. On Sunday morning, at 11:00 A.M. ET, there are on-line religious services for the gender community offered by the Inner Discovery Church, a Universal Life Congregation. The Inner Discovery Church "is a worldwide, non-religious, spiritual support organization, bringing hope, love and acceptance ·to the gender community." You can find transcripts of the services with titles like Getting On-line with God, Grace Under Seige, and Patience to Wait for Your Dreams at this site (http://www.innerdiscovery.org/services.htm). The church preaches belief in one god, finding self-acceptance, learning to let go of fear, and learning to give and receive unconditional love. And of course, the duality of God, embracing both male and female characteristics.

The other large site devoted to gender issues is the **Transgender Forum** (http://www.tgforum.com/). This site tries to cater to all in the transgender community, which is no easy feat. They have a great e-zine published weekly. You can get snippets of it on-line, but a full subscription costs $25.00 annually. If you're a subscriber, you also get TG chat, billed as "no trolls, no harassers, just great conversation and support from and by crossdressers and their friends." There are hosted chats with topics including beginners, sex-change transitions, family life, and discussion for wives and significant others. These chats are ongoing on a weekly basis.

The site is chock-full of information and resources for the transgender community. You can find pictorials, personal ads, TG nightclub listings, ads for friends, a Dr. Nancy advice column, and an extensive library for male-to-female sex-change information. Some resources are available to the public—a limited selection of the library, support group information, organization listings, and regional listings of Web pages. The listing also includes many international groups—it's eye-opening that this is not just an American social phenomenon, but a worldwide way of life.

Here's a snippet from the Dr. Nancy advice column:

Dear Nancy,
I have just discovered (and I'm in my 50s) that wearing women's intimate apparel (garter belt, stockings, high heels) is a tremendous turn-on for me. My mate says that it's no problem for her, but, still, I'm a little uncomfortable wearing these things in her presence. We have a fabulous sex life, and I do NOT want to jeopardize it; can you please give me some reassurance about how women view such things?
—Got a Secret

Dear Got a Secret,
Honestly, different women view things different ways. Personally, I tend to like women who are playful and adventurous enough to enjoy such things. If your wife fits that bill, count yourself lucky and have a good time. Many wives find such things quite confusing, and some are positively revolted. Personally (again), I think it's a "men's liberation" kinda

thing, it should be OK for men to play at being women sometimes, and vice versa. Helps break down barriers.
—Nancy

Learning about transgenderism on the Internet is a way to understand the struggles and joys people who choose to be different have to live through. If you realize you identify as a cross-dresser or transsexual, then you've found a community. If you realize someone in your family or social circle is a closet member of the gender community, you've just become a sympathetic ear. In the privacy of your own home, under an anonymous screen name, you can learn an incredible amount about our fellow human beings and their lives. Resources are available to all.

THE FUTURE OF SEX

Polyamory and transgenderism are things of the present, but what of the future? Rest assured, there are sites out there that are already thinking ahead. Consider the **World Future Society** (http://www.wfs.org). The Society is a nonprofit educational and scientific organization for people interested in how social and technological developments are shaping the future. With 30,000 members, the Society serves as a nonpartisan clearinghouse for ideas about the future, including forecasts, recommendations, alternatives, and more.

In their July/August issue of *The Futurist*, the bimonthly World Future Society magazine, two authors wrote about the future of sexuality. Kenneth Blackwell in "Sex in the Future: Virtuous or Virtual?" believes sexuality will increasingly become a health issue. Discussion about sex will be less inhibited, sexual expression more varied, and sexual health information more available in our future. Sounds like something to look forward to, to me! Joel Snell, on the other hand, writes about sex robots in his article, "Impacts of Robotic Sex." He believes "sexbots" will soon become available, altering social relations. Impacts may include broken marriages, sexbot addiction, experimentation with same-sex sexbots, and the possibility of technovirgins—people who have sex only with sexbots. This one sounds pretty creepy! You can order back issues of *The Futurist* for $7.00 on the site.

Another site that dwells on the future of sexuality as we know it is **Future Sex** (http://www.futuresex.com). They ask the questions, "What do you think sex will be like next year? Next century? Next millennium?" Answers may be found in the Gallery, where new artists are periodically featured with their visual representation of what sex might look like in the future. The art ranges from retro-realism to leather-fantasy. You may also be able to find the answers in the Sci-Fi Arena, where you can read erotica by authors of futuristic science fiction. Titles like "Learn How to Be a Lucid Dreamer," "Lion's World," and "Tunnel 33" depict scenes from the authors' imaginations about how future sex might look and feel. If you're having a psychic and inspired moment, you can send your own fiction to the Web master to be published on the site.

As most of us wonder what the future will bring, it's important to live your present life to the fullest, and, of course, have great sex!

ANNOTATED SITE LISTING

http://world.std.com/~bearpaw/ohp.html The Open Hearts Project collects advice for polyamorous couples.

http://www.playcouples.com The Lifestyles site has an extensive community of sensuous adult couples who swing and swap.

http://www.lovemore.com/ The Loving More site is devoted to exploring alternatives to monogamy.

http://www.polyamory.org The home page for the Usenet newsgroup, alt.polyamory houses a community of polyamory advocates.

http://www.sonic.net/naturat/poly/poly.html A list of people interested in polyamory, with their online contact information.

http://www.tri-ess.com/ Tri-Ess is an organization for hetero cross-dressers and their spouses and significant others.

http://www.gendertalk.com The Online Gender Support Group offers information and resources about gender issues, including the Internet radio show, GenderTalk.

http://www.innerdiscovery.org/services.htm
Transcripts of sermons from the Inner Discovery
Church for the transgendered audience.

http://www.tgforum.com/ The Transgender Forum
caters to all in the transgender community, and
publishes a weekly e-zine including the Dr. Nancy
advice column.

http://www.wfs.org The World Future Society is a
nonprofit organization for people interested in
how social and technological developments are
shaping the future.

http://www.futuresex.com Future Sex dwells on the
future of sexuality as we imagine it.

EPILOGUE

We've covered a lot of ground in *The Joy of Cybersex*. From cyberflirting to polyamory support groups, you've been exposed to a complete range of sexual expression. There's nothing profound about the Internet; in fact, if you've learned anything from reading this book, it's that the Net mirrors our real lives.

While some people do get carried away with the fantasy aspect of the medium (there's no denying it), if you learn how to use the information and interactive tools you find on the Net responsibly, you can greatly enhance your sex and relationships. As a training ground to build skills, the Internet has no rivals. The anonymity and flexibility of the medium allow a safe place to try out new things—anything from flirting to meeting your special someone to exploring your sexual fantasies.

In our society, these are things we're expected to know how to do naturally. And we feel inadequate if we aren't experts. Witness the locker-room discussions about "getting laid" and the tears of women who've been rejected. The truth is, developing healthy intimate relationships and realizing our sexuality potential as singles does *not* come naturally. There are skills and techniques that can be learned—if only someone somewhere would show us how.

The Internet is here. The anonymity of the environment removes any shame and embarrassment associated with sex, and allows us all to be novices and experts at the same time. You can quietly explore things you know nothing about. You can practice new skills with strangers. You can make mistakes, then change your identities to meet new demands. You can become an expert in the art of romance without ever leaving the comfort of your own home. You can explore your sexual fantasies without fear of rejection.

The Internet gives you a chance to find your way without judgment or criticism. It doesn't matter if you haven't slept a wink and have stubble on your face (or on your legs!). The playing field is level; we're all equals in cyberspace.

Armed with an understanding of the range of sexual expression, you're now ready to become a fully sexual being. Whether a sensual single or a hot couple, your newfound knowledge will serve you well. People who are comfortable with sex are sexy. They are more willing to explore and experience their pleasure. They are healthy—in all aspects of their lives. (And yes, they exude a rosy glow and a glint in their eyes . . . whether they've had sex recently or not!)

My hope in being your guide for this material is to make sex an easy, natural topic of conversation. It's time to get sex out from the dusty stacks of our imagination and put it in perspective. Sex is part of a healthy lifestyle; without it, people are miserable. You can tell when people have been celibate for a time (not by choice) or they aren't satisfied sexually in their relationships. They're stressed. Sex is a tension release, it's a stimulant, it gets our juices flowing!

RESOURCES FOR ALL

As the face of the Internet is constantly changing, it's important to know about a few cool Web sites out there that frequently update the links you need to get current sex information.

Tools for Finding Sex Information on the Internet

http://www.viaverde.com/sex/search.htm This site is maintained by Mistress Blanca and Peter and is a meta-index of sexually oriented link lists, search engines, indexes, bibliographies, and catalogs. It's incredibly extensive and regularly updated.

The Society for Human Sexuality

http://www.sexuality.org This site is part of the University of Washington and is renowned as one of the most extensive libraries about human sexuality. Articles are added regularly and cover every aspect of human sexuality that you could think of.

Yahoo's Society and Culture: Sex

http://www.yahoo.com/Society_and_Culture/sexuality
This is the list of lists. It covers all the major subtopics, including General Sexuality, Advice, Activities and Practices, Erotica, Fetishes, and more.

Persian Kitty

http://www.persiankitty.com Persian Kitty is a great compilation of links of adult sites on the Net. It doesn't discriminate between soft and hard porn though, so beware. Categories include Pics, Erotic Stories, Sex Advice, BBS, Chat Rooms, Pay Sites, and more. Most of the sites have a brief description, so you know what you're getting into before you click.

The Complete Internet Sex Resource Guide

http://www.craigsweb.com/netsex.htm If you can get past the pornographic advertisements, this site offers extensive lists of cool Web sites, usenet groups, IRC channels, BBSs, and adult services dedicated to all things sexual. The Web sites are neatly categorized by sex information, personal sites, commercial sites, shopping, phone sex, personals, pictures, and more. Frequently updated, this is a great place to check when you're looking for something specific on the Net.

That's all, folks. I wish each and every one of you happy surfing and wonderful sex.

Index

DEBORAH LEVINE, MA (AKA Delilah): Deb has been answering questions about sex and relationships on the Web for more than five years. At Columbia University, she developed and maintained Go Ask Alice, an award-winning Web site, in addition to providing information to college students, parents, and faculty about safer sex and healthy relationships. At Thrive Partners, Inc., she built and maintained two sites, Thrive@Passion and Love Happens.com, as well as the personality of sex advice columnist Delilah.

A graduate of Cornell University in Ithaca, New York (BSW, 1984) and New York University in New York City (MA, 1991), Deb has used her skills and expertise in a variety of settings throughout the years. Beginning as the coordinator of volunteer counselors for a rape crisis center in Ithaca, she went on to own and manage a vegetarian restaurant, work in the education department of Planned Parenthood, cater for musicians and film crews in New York City, train social service professionals in the metropolitan judicial system, teach conflict resolution to middle school kids, and much, much more.

Currently, she is thirty-five and single, living in San Francisco, California.

Deb has been on national and syndicated radio shows, most recently speaking as the hip Dr. Ruth of cyberspace. She has also, as Alice, been on *NBC Nightly News* and *Now! with Tom Brokaw and Katie Couric*, and has been interviewed for *Computer Life, TV Guide Online, Rolling Stone, Men's Health, Architectural Digest, The New York Times, The Wall Street Journal,* and *Dr. Tom's Guide to Online Medicine,* to name a few. She was also interviewed by President Clinton's advisory council for inclusion in a report on education and the Internet.